The Mayor's Daughter

A Royal Oak Trilogy

T.C. Christman

authorHOUSE®

AuthorHouse™
1663 Liberty Drive
Bloomington, IN 47403
www.authorhouse.com
Phone: 1-800-839-8640

First published by AuthorHouse 5/13/2011

ISBN: 978-1-4520-7265-4 (hc)
ISBN: 978-1-4520-7266-1 (sc)

Library of Congress Control Number: 2011903561

Printed in the United States of America

This book is printed on acid-free paper.

Contents

Acknowledgement

David and Linda Penney, Kathy Maguire, Suzanne Bach,
Marian McCann Rometty, Jack Hayward, Ed Frome, Hugh McLean,
Fred Birchard, Angela Michell, my daughter, Cheryl Marie Michell,
and my beloved husband James Christman.

Introduction

I was born Therese Marie Clawson in the house with the pie shaped lot across from The National Shrine of the Little Flower, 2135 Northwood Blvd. to be exact. When I got married I was Therese Michell. Then in 1987, when I was remarried, I became Therese Christman. My parents, siblings and all my childhood friends called me, "T.C".

The house I was born in across from the Shrine 1926

I grew up in the Northwood Subdivision of Royal Oak, Michigan. U.S.A., an area where the famous talking priest of the 1930's came from, Father Charles E. Coughlin. He was our next door neighbor. My Dad was a realtor, a business he had inherited from his father Dr. Firman William Clawson. My Dad was also Mayor or Commissioner of Royal Oak for about 24 years, and then he turned his efforts to his beloved Beaumont Hospital.

There he spent his remaining years putting his expertise to work for them.

One fascinating item about the town of Royal Oak, Michigan is that it has a direct train route through the middle of the city to Detroit. We have all learned to stop talking when the train goes by, which, by the way, isn't that often

I moved away from home at one point in my life, but due to the plan of God moved back to my parent's home on 2135 Vinsetta Blvd after they had passed away. My husband and I had opened a home for the elderly on 12 Mile Road in 1991, which my husband Jimmy and I had hoped someone in the family would carry on after we were not able to.

Royal Oak had changed a lot in the 45 years I was away. For instance, Royal Oak was always equated with Birmingham, never Ferndale, Madison Heights, and Hazel Park but rather, Birmingham, Cranbrook and Bloomfield, which unconsciously goaded us to be better Royal Oakers.

Birmingham has become miles away from us in 'thinking' and in the newspapers, but not in actual land area. They are still the next town, north, down the street called Woodward Avenue. The two main newspapers "The Daily Tribune" for Royal Oak, run by the Millers and "The Birmingham Eccentric" run by the Averill's made an agreement not to step on each others toes so they would not deliver any Royal Oak Tribunes past 14 Mile road and no Birmingham Eccentrics were to come into Royal Oak. This started the big division between Royal Oak and Birmingham that exists today. When I moved to Birmingham I tried to get the Tribune delivered to us there but I would have to have it mailed to me. Dumb-dee-dumb-dumb! I asked Bill Averill about it one day and he told me about the agreement his father had with Miller. Big mistake for both cities. We needed each other.

The Tribune was so popular at the time of WWII that some families had it mailed to their children in the service. My family sent it to me while I attended college in Florida at Florida Southern College, in Lakeland. Every Thanksgiving day we used to play football against Birmingham High School. What a fantastic game that always was.

Now, we have a local phenomenon started called the "Dream Cruise". This was not a planned event but a spontaneous event. The event seemingly brings Royal Oak and Birmingham closer again than any other event has in years.

I decided that I would take a walk with my dog and see what was happening in Berkley the town across from Royal Oak on Woodward Avenue and 12 Mile Road in the year 2003 on the Friday before the 'Cruise'.

TRILOGY ONE

BOOK ONE
The Dream Cruise

We were making our way down Twelve Mile Road in Royal Oak on the Friday before the 'Dream Cruise' of 2003, just my dog and I. Now, before I go any farther, for those people in "Rio Linda," that is not a trip to the South Seas on a Luxury Liner but a spontaneous reaction by Middle Americans to their love for cars, particularly Detroit area automobile buffs. In some parts of the States you will see boats, but here in Royal Oak you are more apt to see vintage cars and maybe a boat riding along with the rest of the traffic. However, the car takes precedence over the boat in this area of Michigan.

As I understand it, Daniel House, a Ferndale gentleman, started this event (a near-by town on Woodward Avenue next to Royal Oak). He wanted to raise some money for one of the youth clubs in Ferndale. Now in the 40's 50's and 60's the young generation (teenagers) would "cruise" up and down Woodward Avenue going to "car hops", where young girls, maybe even your girl, would come out to your car, sometimes on skates, and serve you a soda pop or ice cream soda, what ever. Coffee was only .10 cents, ice cream .20 cents and root beer float .30 cents, while gasoline was only .15 cents a gallon in the 40's., but for the first part of the 40's it was rationed.

I call this "Dream Cruise" event a "spontaneous combustion", because Mr. House had no idea that the youth of the mid twentieth century would become seniors just ripe for a gathering such as this. They could show off the cars that they had been storing in their extended garages, and let the world see the joy they had in their restored cars, like the ones they used to drive up and down Highway Number 1,

(Woodward Avenue). In 1995, a quarter of a million people turned up for the event and begged they have another next year.

I have years of memories of our Northwood Subdivision. As my dog and I passed various homes along the way, I couldn't help remembering the years lived here and the people I had been raised with, in this close knit community. Marian McCann's house was at the corner Maplewood and 12 mile (called Oakwood then) and the first time I met her, my Dad, who was a land developer in Royal Oak, and his father before him, had started the FW Clawson Land Co., on Woodward Avenue and 12 mile Road. They had developed many of these homes in the 1920's and the 1930's.

DR. F.W. Clawson in light coat, talking with customer
at entrance to Northwood Blvd. Circa 1921.

Another little three year old girl, Marian McCann (and her family) was about to move in very near me. It was all I could do to contain myself, waiting for her to arrive. My Dad had told me that she would be coming in on Friday and I wouldn't let my older sister have any peace until she took me to their house to wait for her.

The Malcolm Jamieson's house in front with Marian
McCann's house being constructed in back.

It seemed forever before they arrived, and there we were on the front porch at 1902, 12 mile, waiting and waiting. At one point my sister Margie insisted that we go home for lunch and I agreed reluctantly. But I could hardly wait to go back to Marian's front porch, a porch I didn't go to very much after that because I used to go to the back door and call for her, "MAAR-EE- ANN", for many years.

We became fast friends and soon her next door neighbor, Malcolm Jamieson, was added to our gang and as well as Barbara Baldwin. Barbara and I had met in another peculiar way. My mother wanted to keep tabs on me as a two and a half year old but still wanted me to "get out in the sunshine" so she would tie me up to the garage door and load me up with toys, sand pails, shovels, etc. One of those summer days I saw a little girl walking with her older sister and I called out to her. She told me she lived down the street on my block (without crossing the street) and that she would come right back and play with me.

What joy! I talked my sister into untying me so I could go inside to talk with mama. Once inside, I told mama all about my new girl friend and that she wasn't tied up and could go all the way around the block, so I should be able to do the same. That was the last time I was tied to the garage door.

We were a unique group of kids living in Northwood.

We grew up during the Great Depression years, next door to Father Charles E. Coughlin and the tiny little Catholic Church that became "The National Shrine of the Little Flower". But when we were kids, it was a little wooden church with a long center aisle and sometimes Father

Coughlin would drop roses from above onto us parishioners. He was charmingly innovative.

This little church burned down on St. Patrick's Day 1936. While we were away in Florida. Someone saved me a beautiful opal rosary, which later I lost.

The 1st. Shrine wooden church after having been moved. Circa 1931.

At this time in our lives we youngsters had no worries. Time was spent growing up and staying out of trouble. Malcolm Jamieson was the adventuresome soul in our group and he would get us into more predicaments than I cared to remember, like the time we soaped the windows on some of our Neighbors houses for Halloween, and of course, we were caught. My mother made me go back and wash Mrs. Smith's window and I remember still feeling so guilty that I baked her some cookies, to tell her I was sorry.

Marian's Fifth Birthday Party. 1st. row left to right, Barbara Baldwin, Malcolm Jamieson, 2 girls and Marian McCann. Sitting in front is Barbara McCann.

My mother wanted me to learn to cook at a young age, so by the time I was thirteen I was preparing the Thanksgiving Turkey all by myself. The only complaint I received was that I had put too much summer savory in grandma's dressing. I wanted it to taste good and my brother teased me about the "sticks" that I had, in the dressing. Mother had gotten fresh herbs from my Aunt Lou's butcher near Wabash Avenue in Detroit, where Grandma Adeline Vallee Herzog lived. Mother and I had dried the fresh summer savory, but when I shook the dried stocks the stems came off with the leaves and thus I had "sticks" in my dressing. What do you expect from a thirteen years old girl?

To be fair to Malcolm, I must admit to occasionally getting him into trouble. Like the time we picked all his mother's tulips and then tried to sell them to her at her front door (This was my smart suggestion). Also, we asked him to get a pencil and he brought out a huge bunch of pencils all rubber-banded together, (his mother was a teacher and very organized) I thought, "They can't possibly have any more pencils in the house, so let's sell them to his mother". Okay that wasn't too bright!

One day, I was talking to Marian about our pencil episode. She reminded me of the time we took all her father's rubber-banded pencils out of his drawer. She sharpened them and went down to the Shrine. She sold some of them to tourists who had come into town to visit "the Church of the Talking Priest". Needless to say, Marian's father was not happy with this action.

The back person is Tom McCann. Left to right the back row Barbara Baldwin, Marian McCann, and in the middle row third from the left is TC. Bottom row second from the left is Patty McCann, and Barbara McCann.

5

Marian's mother would carefully hang her freshly laundered sheets out to dry. This triggered our imaginations. They'd be a perfect stage backdrop! Then we would make up a play for her younger sisters. The story content was never our main object but acting on the stage intrigued us, so we hammed up some screwy story plot, just to be on stage. We tried to charge a penny a seat, but alas no one had any money then, for these were depression years, so finally we let them in free. Malcolm was always the daddy, the soldier, the Indian, or handyman. Bootsie our dog was good for playing the horse, which we never rode because she wouldn't stand up. However, she would allow us to sit on her when she would lie down. Such were our acting careers.

Our drama teacher at Northwood School was Miss Francis Lewis. We adored her. She taught us every thing, even how to file our fingernails properly (going one way only), how to play act and how to have good manners. She became Principal of Northwood School and married after she left Northwood School and became Mrs. Bellefleur. Miss Lewis was really famous for her story telling of "The Secret Garden".

Mrs. Bellefleur formerly Miss Lewis, Northwood School in background.

Many years later she came to spend one night at my home for elderly people and I asked her about the story "The Secret Garden". She said that she had talked it over with the other teachers and they had set a definite point at which they would stop reading each day. Every day we could hardly wait to hear what came next. That is one story that has to be read aloud for you to be spell bound. I have seen two versions of "The Secret Garden" put to a movie and they do not have any of the charm that hearing the words of the book did for us. Years later I met a young man by the name of Bob Taylor, who went to Northwood School and told me of the same happening with Miss Lewis and her reading. This had a big influence on him as a child. He became a writer and wrote for his friend, Tim Allen, on the "Home Improvement" TV series.

Chapter 2
Christmas with Family and Friends

My Aunt Lula would come and take care of me when Mother and Dad went away on a trip. I looked forward to it because she always had suckers for my friends and I. My Dad had developed diabetes and we suddenly had no candy around the house so this was a real treat!

Aunt Lula, my mother's sister whose real name was Louise, was always so sweet to me. She never had any children of her own, but was always kind to me. No matter how obnoxious I was she was always dear to me, and believe me I was obnoxious. I know because my sister used to tell me so all the time. When she said to my Dad, "She's so spoiled"! My Dad's reply was, "No, she just smells that way". My Dad was always funny, that's why my mother loved him, I know.

As Aunt Lula grew old I took care of her and her then husband Louis Tuchell. None of the other cousins paid any attention to them. I guess they never got to know her the way I did. She died at the ripe old age of ninety-two and he died 12 years later at the same age of ninety-two.

Christmas was always a wonderful time of the year for us in our Northwood Subdivision. My Dad, H. Lloyd Clawson, was either a Commissioner or a Mayor of Royal Oak for as long as I could remember. Our subdivision had what we called an auditorium. Now days they call them community centers. I guess he was ahead of his time, because we were the only subdivision with an auditorium and clay tennis courts for the residents to use. The auditorium was available to all in Northwood if they needed it for family gatherings, etc.

Tennis Courts next to Northwood Auditorium.

Hedges second "Wigwam" using Northwood Auditorium.

Later he rented it out to "Hedge", who owned Hedges Restaurant called the "Wigwam". All the kids loved his Wigwam on the corner of Main Street and Woodward. The tables there were like tree limbs for legs, a box top table, stored with moss, twigs, stones, and birch bark, and covered by a thick clear glass. The building was shaped like a giant "Wigwam". It was our favorite place to eat and Brown's creamery was just down the street on Washington Avenue. (David Pressley's School of Cosmetology is there today) and we could get huge three dip ice cream cones for a nickel. For you Royal Oak folks, the closest similar soda shop in existence today, would be Ray's Ice Cream on Coolidge.

In 1931 Dad had arranged to have a Christmas party for the kids and residents of Northwood. Santa would give out candy and cheer people up after the terrible crash of '29. I have a large photograph of all of us standing in front of the big lighted evergreen tree next to the auditorium. The only people I can identify in it are: Me, my father, my sister Margie, my brother Buddy and my cousin Leona and her then husband Earl Cook and my mother, next to them, and Mr. Christie with his bushy eyebrows, I could never forget him. I think Mr. Fred Packard was standing next to my father. He was president of the Northwood association that year.

Celebration at Auditorium for Northwood residents. 1930.

I've often wanted folks to name the other people, but the closest I came was Virginia Merritt, who said about the little girl in the front row, "I had a coat and hat just like that". I believe, Harriet, her sister was that little girl in the front row because she was my age and Virginia was a couple of years younger. I even gave it to Lois Lance to see if she and her sister Betty Rae, or Malcolm Jamieson her brother were in it, but to no avail.

Christmas was a fun time with Santa coming. My Mom went to a lot of trouble, by decorating the Christmas tree in our "sun-room," pretending that Santa was in there helping her. Finally one year I was looking through the key hole and under the door and through every crack I could find to see if I could see Santa Claus, when my killjoy sister came up to me and said, "You're so stupid, there's no Santa Claus. He's just pretend"! Well you might as well have taken God away from me. After that I didn't believe any adult even my mother.....they all lied! I crossed a new road in my life. With that I was determined that no child should be lied to by adults ever again. I tore out of the house and told every kid I knew that there was no Santa Claus. Needless to say I had some mothers very angry at me that Christmas. I ran into

Joanne Crittenden, who several years ago reminded me of how I ruined her mothers Christmas. The kids didn't mind, because they still got their presents but the mothers were furious with me.

On another Christmas the neighborhood had some kind of Christmas pageant at the auditorium and Marian told me that she was the Good Fairy who placed her wand upon my head and the "twins" Joan and Ann Way's heads, then we did a dance after Marian had said, "Wake up little Dolly, wake up little Dolly". It seems that all the children five years old and under in the neighborhood were in this little skit. She said that she never would have remembered this if her mother hadn't been so worried about finding her a magic wand. I think this was a dance recital by Mortimer Hyde. A few years later, the Borgo sisters, Virginia and Frances were our neighbors and used to give me dancing lessons at their home in the subdivision.

Indian Tree on Girl Scout Hill with TC. 1940.

After going to morning Mass, we could open our presents. Then we had hours before we would eat our Christmas turkey dinner, so I would dash off to Marian's house. Barbara Baldwin had to stay home and no friends were allowed because they had a full house with just family, and they didn't need another kid around. But Marian was the oldest of three girls and for some strange reason, they didn't mind me.

That Christmas we compared our Dy-dee Dolls and played with them for many years. I can't believe it but Marian still has her doll. We had more fun (Barbara, Marian and I) that next summer with our dolls under our silver maple tree in the back yard. The doll had a little opening in its mouth where a small bottle with a nipple on it that fit perfectly.

We would fill the bottle with water and when we put the bottle in our dolly's mouth, immediately the doll needed changing. It took us just two times to change the two diapers we had with the kit, for us to start pretending we were giving our dolls water. After all it was all just pretend.

Plowing sidewalks and streets in 1926 Northwood subdivision.

One other Christmas, Thom McCann, Marian's daddy, let me stay, unbeknownst to my mother for Christmas dinner. I was to get two big meals that year, and he gave us a special treat, a glass of wine, which he said that his family always had just at Christmas. My Mom never figured out why I wasn't hungry for dinner, that year. It was fun at Marian's at this season because they always made special cookies with anise seeds in them that they frosted and colored. To this day I make those cookies at my home for the elderly on twelve mile at Cherry-Oak Inn, in Royal Oak. You see, I have not gone very far from my roots even now.

Marians' Christmas Cookie Recipe

2 Cups sugar
1 Cup Shortening
3 Eggs
½ Cup Milk

½ Cup Cream
(Or canned milk)

a pinch of salt
6 teas Baking Powder
6 teas Anise Seeds
6 (about) Cups of Flour-
Enough to nicely
handle dough.

Cream sugar and shortening, add beaten eggs and milk, cream and anise seed. Gradually add flour, baking powder and salt to mixture, until you can nicely handle dough and roll it. Caution: Do not use too much flour or mixture will be brittle. 350 degrees for 10 to 12 min.

Makes about 10 doz.

BUTTER FROSTING

3 Cups Conf. Sugar
¼ to ½ Cups of Butter
3 or 4 Tab. of cream or canned milk

1 teas. vanilla
An egg yoke is optional

Mix sugar and butter, add cream and vanilla.
Use sprinkled sugar to add color

At Christmas time we make them up, and my Ladies at Cherry Oak Inn have fun frosting them. Then they take them home to their children and grand children. So the Christmas Cookie tradition goes on.

Chapter 3
Father Coughlin in My Life

Those were just a few of the wonderful memories that came to my mind walking to the "Dream Cruise" that Friday night, 2003. No one was certain we would even have a Dream Cruise on that Saturday because we had a severe "Black Out". It was over New York, Canada, Ohio and Michigan and none of the gas stations had been open because of it. The Muslim terrorists claimed that they did it and that they won't say how so that they could do it again.

As a child for many years I had walked this walk, but I hadn't done it recently. I guess it was painful to go back, that's why I hadn't been around the Shrine. You have to understand I grew up playing in the parapet that encompasses the tower and housed the lights. The Shrine was growing up as I was growing up, so to speak.

Building the Sanctuary. Circa 1933.

When my Mom took me out of the Shrine School after the third grade, Junior Uhnavy was in my class and I remember asking him what Sister said when I didn't come back. He said that she asked us all to join in a prayer for you. That made me so pleased. I remember my mother discussing who the first baby was christened by Father Coughlin and my mother said I was but someone else said that it was

Junior Uhnavy. Well I know that I was the first Therese christened by Father Coughlin.

Building the Tower of the Crucifix.

I remember listening to a builder describe to someone what their plans were with an altar in the center and pews all around, and how heavy the head of Christ was that was sitting in a box on the outside platform. I was probably about six years old, but I had to tell my grandpa August Herzog what I learned that day, so I gave him a grand tour of the incomplete Shrine. The head weighed five tons, I had no idea what a ton was so, I asked my grandpa and he chuckled and chuckled. I didn't see what he saw as being so funny until years later, but I so greatly wanted to impress him with all the things I had just discovered.

As I was crossing Woodward Ave with my little dog, BiBi, a Bishon, I decided to pick him up, because this had been a long walk for such a little fellow. I stood there on the southwest corner where I could look over at the Shrine. For the first time I realized how beautiful the design was. (It is, to this day, world famous for its "Art Deco" style.) There was a time that the K.K.K. or some group like the K.K.K., burned a cross on the front lawn of the church property, and Father declared openly, "They think they will intimidate me, I will build a big cross they can't burn down"! That's why the tower of the Shrine with Christ on it came into being.

A lot of people said that he, Father Coughlin, hated the Jews but he didn't hate the Jews any more than Americans who weren't Jewish. That was the era that had laws written in the country club by-laws that stated openly that Jews could not join, or on the land deeds that stated gentiles only.

My Dad tried for years to get Jake Levi into Red Run Golf Club, but to no avail. They had been boyhood friends. In this country during WWll we did not know what was happening to the Jewish people in the German occupied countries. It wasn't until after the war that we saw and heard of all the atrocities.

The Jews were smart, they opened their own country clubs, which were more lavish and more beautiful than any of the gentile's country clubs, including, Oakland Hills. When the Women's District Golf tournaments included them in the tournaments, they gave us the best snacks at the ninth hole, fresh fruit. Even the Red Run Golf Course gave us only cheese and crackers at the ninth hole. But wait a minute; I'm getting ahead of myself.

Allow me to go back to the1930's when Father Coughlin was supposed to be so against the Jews. That was the era when signs saying, "for sale Gentiles Only" at Walled Lake and many other locations were posted. Let's face it, it took the holocaust to change the world's and America's behavior towards the Jewish people. But Father Coughlin didn't hate Jews. He was no different than any other American who was not Jewish.

What the Priest hated were the communist and the socialists, who had crept into poor Mexico and tried to make all of the priests and nuns, get married or be killed. This of course, took the lives of all the faithful who had taken a vow to wed Jesus Christ. They closed the Catholic churches and changed them into museums. Many of father's sermons had to do with this subject during those years. He saw that President Roosevelt had let "atheists" into our State Department and they were going to ruin our country, as they had ruined Mexico.

He saw that banks were going to close and that the small investor would lose all their savings, so on one of his broadcasts he warned them of this. Many of them did close, with "the run on the banks". However, some of those small investors were able to get their money out, because they had listened to him.

At this time Father Coughlin disliked F.D.R (Franklin Delano Roosevelt) very much, but it wasn't that way in the beginning before he was President. However, President Hoover was not helping the American men who were out of work. Father Coughlin thought he should help, and because "The Talking Priest" was on the air broadcasting every week, people all over America began to be educated by him as to what was going on in the government. He was like our modern day Rush Limbaugh, or Glen Beck, only he was a catholic priest. Everybody listened to him because those were hard times, people were hurting and he taught them about communism and their atheistic philosophy and the things going on in Washington, D.C. That is why Americans did not like Communists. All through WWII we were skeptical of them.

Father Coughlin wanted so badly to help all the hurting people. He would point out on his program that even a child knew the right answers, so why didn't the government? He would do this by interviewing a child and asking him or her simple questions. Then he would say, "See even a child knows the answer. Why doesn't our government and our President"? My sister Margie was one of those children that he used to interview.

When Roosevelt began to run for President of the United States he got in touch with Father Coughlin, and they became fast friends, so much so, that when Roosevelt made his "Nomination Acceptance Speech" his "Ghost Writer" was Father Coughlin. I know this because the people close to Father waited patiently that nomination night to hear which speech he would read. When they heard it over the radio it was the same speech they had typed out that morning and had given to F.D.R. at the airport. He stopped by to pick it up, and Marian's father was present at this occasion.

Circa 1941. McCann's family in front of Shrine.
Left to right: Barbara, Mildred, Patsy, Thom and Marian.

The term "New Deal" was strictly a Father Coughlin phrase, but he meant it as a good change for America.

After Roosevelt was elected President, Father became very disillusioned with him and started making remarks because the President didn't seem to be stopping the depression and helping the people. President Roosevelt was really carrying out Hoover's plans and taking credit for them as if they were his. Things really got hot and heavy when Roosevelt started to bring in people from communist Russia. Father Coughlin became incensed with these "Godless" people that Roosevelt had asked to come into our marvelously free American country to set up their plans in our State Department. "How could they being atheists help America"? Father would question. He continued complaining on his Radio show until President Roosevelt had him removed from the airwaves. The socialists to this day say that Father Coughlin hated the Jews. No he disliked intensely the atheists, communists and the socialists, plus the Federal Reserve bankers, some of which were Jews.

Chapter 4
H. Lloyd Clawson

The 2003 Dream Cruise Parade in Berkley was now beginning to come out of Roseland Park Cemetery at 12 Mile and Woodward. This has been a tradition (the Friday before the Official Dream Cruise on Saturday) since it first started about eight years ago. I love "L'il old Berkley". It's like family to us here in Royal Oak. None of these cities were laid out for the times we live in now. Royal Oak had two main streets and Berkley had two main cross streets. That's part of their charm. How many parades do you know of that start in a cemetery?

Memorial Day and the Fourth of July parades end up in a cemetery, but we're different in this mid western small town in the good old U.S.A.

The cars proceeded out of the entrance and made a right turn onto 12 Mile Road going west into the heart of Berkley then they would go past a viewing stand and be judged.

Now this "adoration" for these old cars is not new to me. I have grown up around cars all my life. This area at one time was the Auto Capital of the World. You are either a lover of cars or dislike them and are bored with the enthusiasm others have with them. I am enamored with the memory of most of the cars that these enthusiasts seemed to have. I drove many of them at one time or another, even the "1932 Ford Victoria" called the "Vicky", which Don DeWolf, my friend, used to drive when he went to Royal Oak High School. I had a chance to drive. The cars in the late forties, fifties, sixties and seventies were my favorites.

Don DeWolf at 17 in front of ROHS with his 'Vicky' 1932 Ford Victoria.

Back in 1924 the Detroit Free Press wrote an article on August 7th showing a group of people in their straw hats with shovels. It reads, "Governor Groesbeck and a group of State and County officials participated, Wednesday when concrete started pouring into the new paving for "Wider Woodward Avenue". The event marks the beginning of construction on the super highway". Officials shown in the photograph are from left to right; Edward N. Hines, Wayne County Road Commissioner; Frank F. Rogers, State Highway Commissioner; Captain W. S. Gilbraith, Detroit Automobile Club; Governor Groesbeck; H Lloyd Clawson, of the Wider Woodward Avenue Association. (This all happened before I was born, I just happened to have the newspaper clippings about how Dad went up to Lansing to pressure them to act on this decision.)

My Dad's office used to be right across Woodward Avenue in front of the Shrine. The train used to run right by his office when Woodward was a dirt road. So I can see the reason why he was so motivated to correct the Woodward Avenue mess that was there at the present time.

Removing the train tracks on Woodward Avenue in front of Office. 1930

In the thirties I rode in my Dad's cars and I loved the one with the "rumble seat". I remember going with my folks up to Traverse City, to the Cherry Festival and I rode the whole way in the "rumble seat". It was grand fun until my Dad started eating cherries and spitting the seeds out the window. They were hard to dodge and I couldn't let him know what was happening because the window between us did not roll down, so when he stopped for gas I howled at him telling him how tortured I was with that ride. I still wanted to ride in my favorite seat. He laughed and promised not to eat and spit out cherry seeds until we got home.

My Dad's first car Essex 1921.

Then I was happy and we started up again. We had traveled about ten miles when he started to smoke his cigar. Now anyone who knew my Dad knew that he almost always had a "Cigar" in his mouth. In fact, why anyone would buy Dad's used cars I do not know, because they smelled like old cigars, but there we were riding along at a pretty good speed and he started spitting tobacco juice from the cigar out the window. This required quick action on my part to stop from being drowned in tobacco juice and I began pounding on the window again to let him know of my miserable state. After pulling over to the side of the road and finding out what his howling daughter was complaining about now, we agreed I would be happier inside. After that, I only rode in the "rumble seat" when Mom was driving.

Today parents would be considered bad parents for endangering their child and some misunderstanding social worker would want them to be reprimanded for endangering their child. In those fun days, in the wintertime my Dad would hitch the toboggan to the back of his car and pull us up and down the streets. It was the high light of our winter. He would drive around to all the new houses being built in our Northwood subdivision and check on things while we were enjoying ourselves on the long toboggan. Dad, also, would get the fire department to flood the lot next door to the Northwood Fire Station and all of us kids could go skating. I would have my dog Bootsie pull me around on my sled with all the older kids because I was too little to know how to skate.

Chapter 5
The Saturday Dream Cruise 2003

The cars coming onto 12 Mile, were such a variety. There were Scramblers, Mustangs, Studebakers, Buicks, Pontiacs and Fords, and many others that were strange to me. Marian told me that her son-in-law drove a purple Scrambler six years ago and put a purple "Barnie" on top of it. Some of these cars were so funny and they did tricks or had gimmicks on them, like the one I saw a few years ago. There was a car pulling a bathtub with a girl taking a shower in it, in her bathing suit. Then there always was the unhappy resident that just wants to get home from work and gets caught in this traffic.

The Stone at Crooks and Northwood " On this site stood the old homestead of Dr. Firman W. Clawson. The original owner and subdivider of Northwood 'the homestead beautiful' planned and plauted AD-1900."

One of my favorite memories was of something that happened a few years ago. After all the traffic had stopped, around 10: P.M., a paraplegic came out into the middle of the street at 12 Mile and Woodward, in front of the Shrine, he began to do "wheelies" and other tricks that he could do with his chair. He was really great and the folks there all applauded him. He was better than the cruise itself that year.

The best part of the 'Cruise' was that it was so spontaneous. It wasn't organized in any way. It just happened. That's why we all knew no 'black out' would stop it. Everyone who had planned to attend would be there even if they had to camp out the night before, the Dream Cruise. Remember we had no lights, refrigerators, stoves, etc.working. All the old cars had made their way out of the cemetery and west on 12 Mile into Berkley to be judged and viewed by the fans, but I thought it was time for me to go home. As I started to leave my sweet husband showed up to drive us home, stating that he was concerned about our dog, BiBi, (short for Baby Boy). I knew he was worried about me, but he had to have his joke.

Thinking back on those Depression years, we were a creative group of kids. We were restricted in listening to the radio, because our folks loved listening to their own programs. My Dad always listened to "Amos and Andy", and "Lowell Thomas," when he wasn't at the commission meeting. We three children were either playing the piano, drums, saxophone or the radio. My poor Dad had to protect himself from his kids and so he would always sit on his newspaper until he had finished reading it, for we would probably have torn it to shreds with the games, sports and society pages all going in opposite directions.

Circa 1933, in front of Office

During WWII Dad became the "Founding Father" of Beaumont Hospital and was busy starting the hospital authority here in Royal Oak. The two hospitals anywhere around were in the Washington Square Bldg. in Royal Oak, a Doctor's office clinic on Fourteen Mile Road, and a clinic in Ferndale. He knew that we needed one in Royal Oak so he acquired land on 13 Mile Road and got his friends from Red Run Golf Club to start contributing to it. Anyone that wanted to donate was warmly welcomed. Even later on after WWII, when I would be out playing golf with my boy friend and his father, my Dad was soliciting funds for the future Beaumont Hospital. After my brother "Buddy" was killed in England, my father dove headfirst into the hospital project. But I'm getting ahead of myself again.

Groundbreaking ceremony for Beaumont Hospital.
Dad was known for his wide colorful ties.

During the day my Mom would listen for a moment or two to soap operas like "Stella Dallas" or "Ma Perkins". Then she would gripe the rest of the day that she couldn't see how anyone could get anything done if they listened to them for long. We kids loved especially "Little Orphan Annie". They advertised Ovaltine, and we could get a code ring when we sent in for it. Then there was the "Green Hornet" the boys liked, and "The Inner Sanctum", with the Squeeky Door or was that the "Shadow"? Kids of today have all the playthings made for them already, such as dollhouses, playhouses, tree houses and swings. We had an old tree with a big limb that held our swing, and our tree house was a tree on which the boys in the neighborhood built a platform. It was every body's tree house.

The bus that daily drove Northwood residents into Royal Oak and back.

A very special dollhouse was made for me by our gardener, Fred Kazinski, (or was it Fazinski?) for either a Christmas present or a birthday present, but it seemed it was springtime from what I can remember. I let my son's girl's use it and it got lost. Needless to say, I was upset. It was made to look like my house on 2135 Northwood Boulevard. My friends and I used to make curtains for the windows, and the back had a huge door that revealed all the inside. It even had two electric lights and a second floor, and an attic where I could store all the furniture I didn't want to use. I would dress up the dollhouse depending upon the season. Christmas always had a tree and I made wreaths for the windows and front door. At Easter I put on bunny rabbits and little colored candy eggs.

When we weren't playing with my dollhouse or our Dy-dee-Dolls we were making up skits in the back yard for the younger kids to attend for a penny (We were always trying to make some money.) We were Depression kids, and then we would go down to McPeek's gas station at Woodward and 12 Mile Road and buy some penny candy.

Penicillin and television were not invented yet. Neither was Kleenex, or paper napkins. Plastic wrap wasn't even thought of as a handy kitchen item. We still had iceboxes not refrigerators and "hankies". We loved getting ice chips from the milkman or the iceman on hot summer days. There were no air conditioners in houses, cars or businesses. To catch flies we had roll down sticky paper that we hung from the ceiling fans or lights or used fly swatters to catch flies. Somewhere in those years before 'World War II' the refrigerator was installed and the milkman no longer had a horse. However, the ice man still had a horse and would deliver ice to my grandmother in the Detroit area.

On super hot days we would bring our mattresses down stairs to the Northwood side screened in porch and we kids would all sleep together. There was no air conditioning even thought of yet.

From left to right: Bud, Margie, Val, TC and Lloyd
in front of hot weather porch 1932.

Sam Truswell was our milkman. Everyone had a milkman in those days. I believe Sealtest was Sam's company. We never bought milk from the grocery store. We got butter, eggs, milk and all dairy products from our milkman. He was very important to each household. Because Dad was Mayor of Royal Oak, the milkman would ask us, "How many people were coming over for Christmas day dinner"? Then Sam would bring us ice cream Santas or Christmas trees for each person, packed in dry ice. Sam eventually ran for commissioner of Royal Oak and he won. To me that was the beauty of America, everyone has a chance to govern.

My Dad was a very generous man. He gave to the City of Royal Oak the Fire Station at Crooks and Webster, and the land for the Northwood school to the School Board as long as it was used as a school with children in it. He helped pay for the "Trolley" to come into Royal Oak, (I know this because of the big fight my Mom and Dad had about it.) He knew how important it was for the development of Royal Oak to have it run through the downtown area. He cared about his decisions and the effects they would have on the future of Royal Oak.

Northwood school and Jeannie Johnson.

New train tracks in Northwood near 12 Mile Road
1931. Jeannie Johnson loves flowers.

He was the founding father of Wm. Beaumont Hospital. At one point they couldn't come up with a name for the hospital so they offered to name it after my Dad, for $10,000 more in contributions. He never agreed to that, because he never named anything after himself. His father suggested that one street in the subdivision be named after my brother, Lloyd Street. His father named Clawson Street after his family. It just wasn't my Dad's nature to name anything after himself. He named Galpin Street after his friend Fred Galpin, and Smith Street after another friend. Laurome Street was named after Art Laurie and Eddy Frome who were working with Dad when they had to come up with a new name in the subdivision. I believe Vinsetta was a combination of Bassett and Vinton a relative or friend. I heard there is a Clawson Park, which I have never seen. I don't know who named it, but I doubt seriously that it was my Dad.

Fred Galpin with his buck in front of his house. Circa 1910.

He could easily have given them the money but he would never have named anything after himself. That was a vanity that he would never have allowed for himself. Having been raised by a Bible reading "Brethren" father, (my grandfather Firman William eventually became a Presbyterian.) Every day he would read the Bible to his son and his four daughters. Sunday was a day of rest on which they did nothing that was considered work. I never once heard my Dad or my Mom say a swear word when they were angry. My Dad would say "Jumpin Jehoshaphat", but never anything else. My Mom would talk a mile a minute, but swear words never came out of her mouth.

Grandpa Firman William Clawson was a medic in the Civil War. When he returned from the war, he came from New York area to Michigan as a dentist. He was one of the founders of the Wayne State Medical School. His brother, Hibard (who I think they called Barney) went over to the Lansing area and was the first farmer to bring "winter wheat" into Michigan, according to my Dad. The Clawsons still live in the Lansing area. My son who lives there introduced me to a Clawson who had a tile company in Lansing.

On my Dads side of the family, they are traced back to the Revolutionary War. In fact on his mother's side some were English soldiers in the 1600's, so you see my Dad was a man who loved America and what it stood for. His generosity came from the belief that he could never out give God. The more he gave to others the more God gave to him.

Arthur Bassett his child hood friend said one time, "I liked to go into Real Estate with Lloyd. He just knows what's going to make money". He also gave the Congregational Church the land that was the site, of the old farmhouse where he grew up. The farmhouse had burned down in 1917 or 1918. The Northwood Fire Station land which he gave to Royal Oak is now the Royal Oak Historical Museum.

Dr. F.W. Clawson's farm house on Crooks Rd.

New Northwood Fire Station.

The land next to the fire station was where he grew up as a boy in 1898 and is where the Congregational Church on Webster and Crooks Road is now located. He gave them this property, in memory of his sister Ina, who was married to Dr. Chas. Ernest Clark in June of 1903 and they went right to Sivas, Turkey. They had been missionaries in Turkey for just short of 40 years of their life, and were members of the Congregational Church. It was a very hard life for them, but they never complained. They had five children Ruth, David, James, Steven and Connie. When each child was still young they would school them where they lived in Sivas until the child was ready for high school then they would bring him or her back to the States and place the child into a special school for missionary's children. However before World War I the Turks came against the Armenians because the Armenians were for the Germans and the beginning of the Armenian Genocide started. The Armenians were friends with the Missionaries, and that forced the Missionaries to flee Turkey.

The Charles Ernest Clark Family-Ruth is Oldest girl,
and baby girl is Connie in Aunt Ina's lap.

I would like to tell you a story that my cousin Ruth wrote to her
Great Grandson in 1998 about this incident.

...... *"We lived in a compound. My father was the chief doctor.*

He would go out to the villages, sometimes in ox carts, to see his patients. Sometimes I was allowed to go with him. I didn't attend school, but was taught by one of the missionary ladies, Miss Rice. There was a boarding school in the compound. I would occasionally get to play with those older children. Usually my friends would be the Armenian servants' children. A terrible thing happened to my friends from Armenia. One day my friends thought they were going on a picnic, but the Turks, who were at war with Armenia, sent them to the desert. They never came back...... One day they told us we had to return to America immediately. The Turks were coming to get my Dad because my parents hid Armenians in the compound. I left all my toys with the servants saying I would return to get them. We went by ship to Auburndale, Massachusetts. I was seven years old.

Signed, Ruth Clark Ruesink

A wonderful family tradition was started in the Ruesink's lives. When Ruth came back to Michigan she had no toys at all so her Aunt Edna went out and bought her a beautiful doll. She cherished it so much that she gave it to her daughter Barbara when she was seven and Barbara's daughter in turn gave it to her daughter when she was seven. The Armenian genocide is not forgotten in a little girl's doll.

Aunt Edith one of my Dad's sisters married Rev. Robert Clark, Dr. Chas. Ernest Clark's brother...So we had two Clawsons married to two Clarks.

Miss Edna Clawson after graduating from U of M.

My Dad's two other sisters were Mary Louise, known as Louise, and Edna. Life was difficult for them also because World War I came along and Aunt Edna's beau was killed in that war and Aunt Louise's beau died from "consumption" after the war. They were both school teachers with degrees from U of M, for Edna and MSU for Louise, or as Aunt Louise would fondly say, "Moo U". Aunt Louise was only nineteen when she taught school first in a one-room schoolhouse. All of my Dad's sisters were college graduates. My grandfather's sister LaVeena believed that all women should have a college education, so she paid for them to attend the college of their choice.

Miss Mary Louise Clawson graduated from MSU.

My Dad was a very generous man that was demonstrated by all the things he did for everyone. He would pay for all the students of Northwood School to attend the Shrine Circus, and charter the buses to take them there (and in those days we were allowed to ride the elephants). Lois Lance tells me that he also paid for every student to go to "Orchestra Hall" to see the plays like, "Rip van Winkle", "Rumple Stiltskin" or "Beauty and the Beast". Those were depression years and many parents didn't have the extra money to pay for their children to attend such a frivolity. I remember as a little kid finding out that some of my classmates couldn't attend the musical plays and I begged my Dad for them to go too and they did.

The Dream Cruise was over now and the memories that had flooded my mind while I enjoyed the 'Cruise' had inspired me to write them down. My memories of Father Coughlin, and my Dad H. Lloyd Clawson were many. These were two different men one who changed the course of America's political future, and the other who helped form the City of Royal Oak, Michigan during the Great Depression years, and became the founding father of Beaumont Hospital.

THE END OF BOOK ONE

Woodward Avenue, 12 Mile Road and Northwood Blvd.

BY: T C Christman

TRILLOGY TWO

BOOK TWO
The Man Who Gave Too Much

This is a living story of a wonderful man who loved people. I say it is a living story because it is the story of many, many American families across this great country. It is similar to so many people who were part of the greatness of America and left a legacy for those who never knew them. They were the God fearing people who were not ashamed to say they believed in a living God who watched over them and guided them through their lives, through thick and thin, through good times and bad. These were people who made America great, and knew the God of Abraham, Isaac, and Jacob, who loved them.

Henry Lloyd Clawson in 1906.

Where do you start when you want to share one special life that was so beneficial to a small Midwestern town in Michigan? I suppose, the only logical way is to start with the facts of this person's life.

Mayor H. Lloyd Clawson and commissioners. November 6, 1929.

Many mayors have come and gone and each mayor or commissioner of small towns such as Royal Oak contributed their very best. It is a difficult job and each mayor or commissioner can look back over their years in office and say "I tried to protect my city from future problems and current problems, and to incorporate future resources for good growth". Such was the mayor I want to tell you about. His name was Henry Lloyd Clawson, better known as H. Lloyd Clawson. The city of Clawson was indirectly named after him, so I will veer off course to tell you how that came into being.

Clyde Lawson from Lawson Lumber Company.

Lloyd had a boy hood friend whose name was Clyde and his family ran a lumber company. One day Clyde was disgusted with having to go all the way to the Post Office in Royal Oak. His business was located on 14 Mile Road near Main Street in Royal Oak Township, so to expedite time, for many of his orders were coming by mail, he went to Lansing to have packages delivered directly to his business. When all the paper work was filled out, everyone including Clyde, discovered they had a new town called Clawson. My dad went right over to Clyde and thanked him. They for many years laughed and laughed about how my dad had managed to have a city named after him. You see, Clyde Lawson had signed the papers   C Lawson.

To begin Dad's life, it was March 13th, 1888, and the Michigan weather was terrible. The people of that era called it the Blizzard of '88. This child was the first boy in a family of five children, so to speak he had four MOTHERS (one real mother and three sisters who acted like they were his mother) and one sister who was like a twin, Louise, who was born one year after him. His parents and sisters said many prayers when he was tiny because he was not a sturdy baby and they were not sure that he would live, plus the fact, that he was a boy and not at all like his sweet little sisters. As time went on he found himself in many strange and dangerous situations and as his mother used to say, "But for the Grace of God" he would not have made it out alive.

F.W. Clawson children left to right clockwise: Ina, Edith, Edna, Baby Louise and Lloyd.

Lloyd's father was a dentist in Detroit who taught at the Detroit Dental College, a fore- runner of the Wayne State Medical School. Dentists often did the work of doctors in the early days of medicine.

Firman William Clawson, Lloyd's father, was honorably discharged from the Civil War as a medic. He went on to become a dentist and his older brother Charles became a doctor in New York after the War. This information can be found in Leslie L. Hanawalt's book, "The History of Wayne State University 'A Place of Light" also in the Medical Biography of Seneca County, New York.

"Bill" Clawson's family left to right top right: Edna, Charles Ernest Clark, Ina Clawson Clark, and Edith. Front row left to right: Lloyd, Mary Elizabeth Van Liew Clawson, F.W.(Bill), and Mary Louise Clawson.

His father, F.W.Clawson, known as Bill, was from a Revolutionary War family. His grandfather was only nine years old when he fought and his mother Mary Elizabeth Van Liew was from the Osgood Family whose lineage goes back to before the Salem 'Witch Hunt' years. They were British soldiers stationed here with their families.

I will give you a little run down on one of H. Lloyd's great, great, etc. grandmothers whose name was Mary Clement Osgood. Her husband was a well-liked British soldier. She had 12 children. Of these three had died; the last one a few years before this incident took place. It seems that Mary (Clement) Osgood, born in 1637, England, daughter of Mr. Robert Clement of Haverhill, married a very popular military man, Sergeant John Osgood II on November 15, 1653.

He later became a lieutenant and then a captain. His father was the original proprietor of Andover. "In 1692, Mary was about 55 years old, and through lineage and marriage, was one of the three highest ranking women of Andover". She and John were both members of the Puritan Church. They had twelve children. Three died young, and three lived

43

at home and six were married into equally prominent families, when this incident happened.

John Osgood Senior was second only to Mr. Simon Bradstreet in the founding of Andover in 1643. He was one of ten founders of the Church in 1645, and Andover's First Representative to the General Court. He died unexpectedly of influenza in his mid- 50's and the heritage fell to his elder son John, Junior, 21 years old.

John Osgood Jr. took on the responsibility of his wife and young family and also his mother, sisters, and younger brother, as well as the civic responsibility of a developing community. Between 1670 and 1690, he served14 times as Selectman, and with Thomas Chandler and Dudley Bradstreet, he alternated as Andover's Representative to the General Court.

Unable to attack John Osgood Jr. directly, the accusers, who were the elders in the Puritan church, went after his wife and the extended family members. An irony of the situation in 1692 was that Mary's son Peter, was serving as a constable of Salem, and in that position had to arrest his mother as a witch, and many of the accused soldier's family members of Salem".

This is information from the Archives of the Andover records in Salem about the Witchcraft Trials. In my words the reason why they accused her was because her husband was such a prominent citizen and they could not attack him. It seems that the French Indian War was going on and the Indians were attacking the citizens too close to home and the soldiers did not want to leave their families unprotected by leaving to fight in Canada. The decision not to go to Canada to fight the Indians was made by John Osgood Jr. so the Puritan Rulers called this "insubordination," and rallied to 'get' him. This comes from 'The Devil Discovered' by Enders A Robinson.

This is one of the character building stories of life that influence a young boy. His mother would relate these stories that she had heard as a child, perhaps on cold and dreary nights, how Great, Great Grandpa Osgood had paid for his wife and others to get out of prison, when the Elders had turned against him.

They had manufactured and manipulated reasons to claim that she was a witch. Grandpa Osgood had stood his ground, but died soon after of a broken heart, that his own Church Elders had turned against him.

Chapter 2
Lloyd Clawson Growing Up

F.W.(Bill) Clawson, who was my Grandfather, found that the country living gave him and his family better health so he moved his family from Detroit to the Township of Royal Oak when Lloyd was about 10 years old. Their farm house was located on Crooks Road where the First Congregational Church of Royal Oak now resides. (The grateful people of the Congregational Church made a bowl out of the apple tree that was in the front yard and a pin and earrings out of the wood from the maple tree in their front yard. I still have the pin set but the bowl was lost in moving.)

DUR going down Woodward Avenue after a heavy rain in 1902.

DUR at Woodward near 12 Mile Road. Circa 1921.

F.W. would still travel every day to his office in Detroit, by way of the DUR (the electric car and later the train) which ran down the dirt road Woodward Avenue from Birmingham to Detroit... He also would teach at the Wayne Dental School every day but Sunday, the Lords Day.

Train accident on Woodward and 11 Mile Road. Circa 1902.

Their next door neighbors were the black family named Hamer (pronounced Hay-mer.) Their daughter "Minny" used to play with my Aunt Louise. They lived across Crooks Road. They even had slumber parties together. The Starr Family gave them a few acres of land, after the Civil War where the Oak Ridge Market is located on Crooks Road today. She went to school with Edna, Louise and Lloyd, at 13 mile and Crooks Road.

Physics lab class circa 1906. Piety Hill, Birmingham.

Back row left to right: Blanche Lowry Claxton, Jean Purdy, Bessie Schuller, Janita Plumstead, Cary Davenport, Lillian Stauch, May Erwin, Charles Streeter, Harry Rodgers, Vernon McDonald, Mr. Bellis, Elmer Haack, Ellis Green.

Front row left to right: Aline Harbison, M. Louise Clawson, Frank Walker and H. Lloyd Clawson.

Graduating class circa 1906. Lloyd Clawson is the 4th student
on the right hand side of the end desks and his sister Louise
is the 2nd girl down from the top row on the right hand side
with Charlie Randell next to her. Piety Hill, B'ham.

Lloyd and his little sister Louise were like twins. They were in the
same grade and went to the same schools, Birmingham High School.
Birmingham was called "Piety Hill" at that time and the direct route
was down Woodward Avenue to Maple road (15 mile road.)

Looking south down Woodward Avenue at 13 Mile Road.
Trees are in Mrs. Parker's yard. Circa 1910.

There was a time, when Aunt Louise and I were going by the Beaumont corner, 13 Mile Road and Woodward Avenue on the south west corner, where she pointed to a spot (which was all highways) where she and my Dad were riding their sleigh too fast on the way to school. They got "up sot," she said, and landed in Mrs. Parker's strawberry patch. To this day, I can't go by that Beaumont corner without thinking of two kids turning over their horse and sleigh in the snow on their way to school and laughing about it all the way to school. They would stable their horse in the barn (a spot that is now the Birmingham Post Office).

Wood planked Road 12 Mile Road in 1902 at Woodward.

One time their father took them to the edge of their property on Woodward Avenue and pointed out the direction of Pontiac (north) and the direction of Detroit (south). The railroad went both ways and the road was a plank lined dirt road and he said to them, "Luiza and Lloyd, someday this road will be lined with houses and stores from Detroit to Pontiac". She said that her dad's nick-name for her was "Luiza".

Louise and Miss Mary in front of Benjamin's House. Circa 1897.

Aunt Louise told me of another time when she was twelve and Dad was thirteen and they went down the "Saw Dust Trail". I had never heard this term before and she explained that the Methodist Church in Royal Oak was having a Tent Revival Meeting and the floor is covered with sawdust, to prevent muddying up the people's feet or clothes. When the "Altar Call" is given and people go forward as God moves their hearts they sometimes kneel down and receive Jesus as THEIR PERSONAL Lord, and because of the sawdust, they don't get dirty.

Now their Dad was a devout Plymouth Brethren, who later turned Presbyterian. Every day before they went to school or did anything, he read the Bible to them. Sunday was always the Lord's Day and no work was done unless it was an emergency. They would look at stereopticons of the Holy Land and dream of what it must have been like in the time of Jesus. I still have these today.

On Sundays, no one was allowed to do any work, so they had servant girls to do their work if anything really needed to be done. How he rationalized this I could not figure out, but that was my Grandpa. However, to be honest about these actions a lot of people in this era did not work on the "Sabath," if they could afford it.

My Dad's childhood friend was a fellow by the name of Charley Randell. They did a lot of travelling and had many escapades together as they grew up. I have two pictures taken around 1905 of their classroom setting in Hill School Birmingham. Charley and Louise are in both of them along with Lloyd and various other classmates. Before Dad was married in 1917 he travelled to the Grand Canyon with his boyhood friend Charley and Alex (or John) Mac Donald. Then Charley went into World War I, something that Dad could not do because of his poor eyesight.

Charlie Randell in uniform of World War I.

The Grand Canyon left to right:Charles Randell,
John(or Alec) McDonald and H. Lloyd Clawson.

Lloyd Clawson and Charlie Randell his best man in 1917.

Charlie Randell left to right: Lloyd on donkey, And unknown friend.

My Dad's first job outside the family work was as a short order cook in Highland Park, Michigan. At that time this was a "posh" town of wealthy individuals. He worked at a small restaurant on Woodward Avenue and his father was his first customer. This was one of the few stories Dad told me about himself.

Dad married LaVallee O. Herzog on June 30,1917 with Charley B Randell and Madaline Wright as witnesses. They were married by Pastor Father Doherty at St. Vincents in Detroit. Father Doherty said to my mother, "Don't try and make him be a Catholic, for he's a fine man who loves God".

LaVallee ODella Herzog future Mrs. H. Lloyd Clawson.

Chapter 3
Starting Political Life

Early Royal Oak was only a Township and I have a picture of my Dad, Lloyd Clawson, holding a tea kettle with George Dondero in back of him and eight other gentlemen standing next to him with a sign that reads ROYAL OAK TOWNSHIP. Below this picture is another showing a station wagon type car with the words SILVERSOUND on its spare tire, and four or five blaring horns on top to draw attention to it. Near it are two ladies, one a nurse and the other looks like a Salvation Army lady. A gentleman is holding the door and above his head a sign reads, "EXTRA DOLLAR CLUB" and smaller letters read, "Detroit Community fund please help put it over". It must have something to do with World War 1.

Note George Dondero in back of Lloyd.

In 1924 at the age of 36, Lloyd became a commissioner of Royal Oak replacing Walter D. Clark, who had become ill and retired. Royal Oak became a city only three years before. The mayor at that time was George Dondero.

In 1921 Lloyd Clawson was enthusiastically pushing for the widening of Woodward Avenue which had a train track going through Royal Oak and then down Woodward into Birmingham. Ever since 1895 there has been an electric car system from Detroit to Birmingham down Woodward Avenue, called the DUR.

DRU workers 1902 on Woodward Avenue "gent with Mutton Chops Whiskers is Mr. Jenson."

H.Lloyd Clawson had been elected City Commissioner in 1924. On August 7th, 1924 Gov. Groesbeck, with Mr. Clawson near him, in a grand ceremony, turned over the first dirt to begin the construction of the superhighway of Woodward Avenue. Aren't we glad we have that terrific boulevard when the "Dream Cruise" comes around? There are some people who are grouchy about any new thing or any event that takes place in the world. For those who enjoy the "Dream Cruise", I say," Go For It"!

Bad timing came after Lloyd was elected the first time to be Mayor of Royal Oak, when the Great Crash of 1929 came and all people felt the terrible uncertainty of each day. This created anguish for Royal Oak residents and Michiganders, so as mayor, he went up to Lansing, to see what could be done, as he would do many times in his tenure.

An appeal had been drafted by the commissioners to relieve property owners of high taxes. He requested that Governor Brucker call a special session of the legislatures to consider this suggestion. Mayor Clawson declared high taxes were one of the obstacles to commercial prosperity. He suggested that the state take over all main paved streets running through cities, connecting state highways and assume all special assessments coming due. He also suggests the state take over trunk line, sewers and drains, serving large areas and also assume unpaid obligations.

An Article in the news paper titled PLANNING, stated that Mayor Lodge (sic) Clawson of Royal Oak, "has called a joint meeting of city commissioners with the four Oakland County supervisors who represent the city. Relieving unemployment and a new plan for refinancing the city over a five-year period will be studied".

The Royal Oak Boy Scout Troup 14 called the Rovers made History for lasting so long according to the Scoutmaster Robert Snelling. The purpose of the trip was to give the boys "extended camping experience". The group of 8 teenagers and 2 leaders left Royal Oak for Yellowstone National Park traveling 4,100 miles in 23 days round trip. Mayor H. Lloyd Clawson and the commissioners had appointed them official representatives of the city by a resolution and provided them with a special banner for their station wagon. For more details go to Twigs and Acorns by David Penney and Lois Lance. Page 202

Left to right " Bud"(Lloyd Firman), H. Lloyd Clawson,
"TC" Clawson, Val and Margie. 1929.

A proclamation asking for the cessation of business from noon until 3 o'clock on Good Friday was issued by Mayor H. Lloyd Clawson for April the 18, 1930. "Whereas, Friday, April of this year being Good Friday, and whereas, throughout the Christian World prayers of sorrow and reverence are held on that day to commemorate the Crucifixion of Jesus Christ our Savior. Therefore, I, H. Lloyd Clawson, mayor of the city of Royal Oak, do proclaim the hours from 12:00 0'clock noon until 3:00 p.m. on that day shall be hours of prayer and I ask that all business be suspended. I urge our citizens to attend the various services held throughout the city that we may silently unite in prayer and meditation".

On Wednesday June 3, 1931 the first D.S.R. Car (Detroit Street Railways Car) was welcomed to Royal Oak. Mayor Clawson and city commissioner Fred Cowen with Lloyd's son Buddy, helped to run the car as far as Royal Oak. Up until then, the car only ran to Eight Mile Road. By payment of $12,000 cash and agreeing to forget about back personal taxes due, Royal Oak acquired the tracks from the Eight-Mile road to Catalpa and Main street. The venture was profitable for Royal Oak at a rental of $5,000 a year.

In 1934, Detroit Mayor Couzens put together a subway committee and they held their first formal meeting on March 2, Friday. They were to make preparations to go to Washington, DC, to urge Federal approval of the project. Col. Waldon was the chairman, and the mayors of four cities around Detroit, made up the committee: Mr. Markland of Highland Park; Clyde Ford of Dearborn; Lloyd Clawson of Royal Oak; and Mr. Degenhardt of Ferndale. It evidently didn't work out, because we heard no more about it. We did have the train going through Northwood Subdivision and on to Birmingham from Royal Oak, which was used by many to reach Detroit before and during the World War II era.

Grand Trunk Train at Northwood Station 12 Mile.
Gov. Bruckner with hat in hand 1931.

In Grand Rapids on April 19, 1934, the P.T.A. headed by A. R. Jamieson introduced a resolution backed by the Southern Oakland County associations. The schools did not have enough money to carry on past Christmas. Quick action was needed to prevent further problems. The home owners could not be taxed more and action was needed, so Mr. Jamieson (Lois Lance's father) and my father went to Lansing to get the problem resolved. An agreement with the banks was worked out so that the home owners paid their taxes later and the banks did not foreclose.

The graduates of ROHS left to right: Bud, Fred Linscheid, Pete Smith and Johnny White 1936.

H. Lloyd Clawson served 2 terms on the school board about the time that he became a Commissioner. He served 4 terms from 1929 to 1937 as Mayor during the Great Depression, and then as Commissioner five terms. He gave back to Congressman George Dondero the gavel that Dondero had used as Royal Oaks first Mayor. Upon Congressman Dondero's death in 1968 his son Robert gave the Gavel to the Royal Oak Historical Archives on March 13, 1969. A line in the 1939 letter from Mr. Clawson to Congressman Dondero read as follows: "Thanks for …..allowing me to use this gavel, I'm returning it….and I trust it will always be available on occasions of this kind and as long as the City of Royal Oak is a thriving and progressive community".

Humor at the commission meeting.

My Dad, Lloyd had a wonderful sense of humor, which made him very popular. He never insulted or put anyone down, but instead would help them get out of a predicament or an embarrassing situation. All of the men on his commission were his friends. He would always be there for them if they needed him. When meetings began to get too hot with arguments he had a way of dissipating the problem with a quick joke that would get everyone laughing and change the atmosphere immediately. People enjoyed being around him because he was always so cheerful. He loved people and he loved Royal Oak.

As a young child I can remember a couple of funny things he said to me that really had me chuckling every time I thought of them. The first one was one time he and I were wrestling and he was trying to tickle me and I was trying to tickle him. When I discovered he was ticklish and I yelled out to him, "You're ticklish"! and he replied back just as fast, "No, I'm Presbyterian"! I stopped and looked at him and said, "What's a Presbyterian"? I had no idea what he was talking about.

Later on I went to camp, and fell in love with horses. I looked forward to camp just to ride the horses. I so wanted a horse of my own. My brother had Ned and I just had to have one, so day in and day out I would talk to my Dad about getting me a horse.

TC on Ned 1931.

Finally, he had just had enough, so he said to me, "Okay, when we move to California I'll get you a horse, any kind you want". That's all I needed to know and I was happy. I never harassed him again about buying me a horse. I told Marian's father and he said, "Are you moving to California"? My answer was, "Someday". I finally realized I had been taken! Our lives were tied to Royal Oak and we would never leave. My dad and his sense of humor again.

Another time my sister came to him and said, "She's so spoiled"! (Referring to me) and Dad's reply was, "No, she just smells that way"! I laughed for years over that one. Another was (when I was grown up) someone asked my dad how tall he was. He replied, "Five foot three". And I stupidly said, (thinking in age he had lost inches and knowing that I was only five foot three) I asked, "How tall did you used to be"? And without a second passing he said '"Six feet"! Needless to say we all laughed for hours over that.

There was a time when he was Mayor that the Police Chief told him they had captured a man from (I believe) The Black Legion. This man confessed that he was sent to kill the Mayor of Royal Oak, but he couldn't do it. He said that he had stood over his sleeping body in his Royal Oak home for several minutes, but he couldn't pull the trigger.

In 1941 he became enthusiastic about a hospital in Royal Oak. Every where he went he talked about it. He had his daughter, (me,) who was taking art classes do a drawing of a hospital for him to use. (Miss Harriet Medes was my art teacher then from Clara Barton Jr. High School.) He would play golf and spend all of his time talking about the future hospital. Many of the first donors were members of Red Run Golf Club.

I remember talking to Miss Medes about the fact that Dad wanted me to do a drawing of a Hospital. We argued about it because I felt very inadequate to produce such a rendition, she convinced me that she would walk me through the various steps needed to produce this building. You have to realize that I only wanted to do portraits or still life's, not buildings, especially hospitals.

Harriet Medes in Deerfield, FLA. with her orange tree.

The next week when I returned for my lesson she had a thick, thick piece of poster board all ready to work on. I had so hoped she would forget what I had mentioned to her the week before. She commenced to teach me about perspectives and the relationship to the horizon. I had to make all the decisions myself she refused to make them. Like, "How high do you want the door? Do you want one door or two? What about the windows"? she asked. That question struck a cord with me. I immediately said I disliked little windows, in fact to be exact I said I hate little windows! She said, "You don't have to have little windows. You can have any size you want". I told her that I would like long windows, but I didn't know how they could build them because of the rooms. Her reply to me was, "Don't worry about that. You just want your building to look good for the drawing…let an architect worry about that". I put in the long windows in the front of my building. I noticed the other day that the first part built of Beaumont had those long windows.

I don't remember what I did for the first floor next to the door. However, I remember talking to her about the left side of the building where I placed the front door and that I didn't want any windows on that side of the building. I didn't like the looks of windows on that side but I didn't want to leave it plain. So she told me, "You can have a bas relief of some design on the brick". I liked that idea but what I came up with I cannot remember. After we had finished my drawing for my Dad I gave it to him. He seemed please but I never heard about it or saw it again.

In 1941, World War II started on December 7th and he felt an even more urgent need for a hospital. The only hospital that Royal Oak had was in the Washington Square Bldg., which I believe he and Art Bassett owned. It was very small and was on the third or fourth floor. Another hospital was on 14 Mile Road (I believe a doctors clinic) plus a clinic in Ferndale. He was going down to Ford Hospital in Detroit for his eye exam to Dr. Ruddeman. They would spend most of his time talking about the future hospital. He learned firsthand the problem that Ford Hospital had, which was "no area to grow". He envisioned a hospital that could do all kinds of services, not only for patients but for teaching and even creative inventive devices, so they must have lots of land. He later told me that the greatest thing he thought he had done for the new hospital was convincing the Board to buy the extra land.

My brother Bud had enlisted in the Army and went on into the Army Air Corp. When he left for basic training, I was away at a new camp. Doug Light, a classmate of mine from Northwood School, had lost his father that year and his mother wanted to have a summer camp for all the girls my age with her older daughter, Florence, supervising. It was really a great idea because there were several grade schools in Royal Oak and we were all going to be in the same classes at junior high and none of us knew each other. Only the ones from Northwood were acquainted with one another.

7th Grade Class 1940 Northwood School.

1st Row: Pickton, Corbin, Stiles, Patrick, Stock, Libby, Pilson, Reynolds, Harding, Green.

2nd Row: Jamieson, Johnson, McClelland, Munro, Bonar, Troxler, Clawson, McPhee, Little, McPhee, Luebs, Easton.

3rd Row: Giles, Walsh, Phelps, Hamilton, Shannon, Hess, Waugh, Steigleder, Parker, Taylor.

4th Row: Light, Baldwin, Iuppenlatz, Rauchle, St. Clair, Igel, Melvin, Rastenburg, McClure, Drake.

My Mom was so sad about my brother going into the service that she talked my Dad into picking me up from camp so I could be home with them. My Dad had driven such a long way to bring me home that I couldn't say "no". I sensed he was hurting too.

At that time it was also necessary to write Bud a couple of letters a day. Dad knew that "Mother" (a name Dad always called her) would write at least two a day so he figured if he wrote some shorter ones that maybe one or both of the letters would get to him. Bud had asked for some candy and razor blades. The only candy Dad could find that could be sent and be the safe to package were some Tootsie Rolls. Dad said that he packaged them all together and sent them with a note, " be careful not to eat the razor blades". This was Dad's sense of humor.

Bud Clawson and Jack Lawson 1943.

Bud graduated as a pilot from Blythville, Arkansas in 1943. I took a picture of him coming down the stairs with his new friends, one of whom was Elmo. I've never seen a happier group of guys. By August of 1943 they were all at Fort Bragg, North Carolina.

March 25, 1943, Blythville, Arkansas Coming down stairs at the
Noble Hotel left to Right: Ed, Bud, Okie, Hamilton and Cisar.

Then in October, they were transferred to Baer Field, Fort Wayne,
Indiana, and a little closer to home.

Top row left to right: "Okie", TC, Hamilton, Bottom row: Bud and Ed

Bud was now thinking of marrying Helen Lawson, Clyde's youngest daughter. He was able to make a few stops at the Pontiac Airport. He said that they were so surprised to see a C47 or DC3 come to their little airport. He said he made history for them. He also was known for BUZZING the men at Red Run Golf Course on his return to his base. He found himself doing more things with his friend Elmo. (Their buddies called Eddie Frome, Elmo; Buddy they called Duke.)

Last family photograph with Helen Lawson, Bud's fiancé 1943.

The winter of January, 1943 was snowy and cold and Dad wrote Bud that he was exhausted from all the shoveling he had to do, because Carl our handy man, was sick and unable to do it, but true to the unevenness of Michigan weather, the January of 1944 was so mild that Dad thought he would be able to have a picnic outside.

In some of the letters I have, my Dad mentioned the land he and his sisters owned in Calabasis (I think that's the name), California on Ventura Blvd. 280 acres, in San Fernando Valley. I later gave the mineral rights to Wm. Beaumont Hospital from my Aunt Louise's estate and no one knows what happened to them. Dad had sold the land to Bob Hope, but kept the mineral rights for his sister Louise. Beaumont has never even mentioned her name in their long list of contributors, which made me very sad.

Ranch for sale with Louise Clawson and friend below the sign.

Ventura Blvd. next to ranch sold to Bob Hope.

Dad mentioned to Bud about the future hospital plans in his Tuesday January 11, 1944 letter #20, "Of course last night, Monday night, was my commission night and nothing too exciting is happening in the City affairs, however the realization of a nice, large new hospital for Southern Oakland County is in the formation period and is taking a lot of time, in fact we have to have some State Legislation, which might take 12 months to get through. We are conferring with the Governor on it and he might possibly help out by putting it in their special session that they are holding this month. That would reduce the time considerably, and yours truly is chairman of that committee and spending a lot of time on it, but if we can accomplish a nice hospital, the best in this locality, I will have done my share".

Another letter from Dad to Bud dated February 7, 1944. #28 said, "Tomorrow, I have to go to Lansing on our Hospital Committee work, of which I happen to be chairman. We are going to see if we can get the legislature put through legislation, which is now in special session. We are anxious to get all of this primary work done in advance, so that we can get to the actual construction of the hospital as soon as the government will permit, which will probably be after the war. It looks now from all indications that we will have to build a two to four hundred bed hospital in order to take care of the area which it will have to serve. The location has not been determined, but the way it looks now, it will be somewhere near Woodward and 13 Mile Road, near Father Coughlin's School that he built up near the Parker School. I think you will recall the location".

Little did he know that while he was in Lansing working for the Hospital Authority Committee his only son was in a fatal accident in England. His world would now change drastically.

Chapter 4
The Horrors of War

The horrors of the war hit home on February 8th, 1944 when his only son, "Bud" (Lloyd Firman) was killed in a plane accident in England. His family completely fell apart at this time. His wife had to be hospitalized because she didn't want to live. His oldest daughter, Margie, had a mental breakdown and no doctor knew what it was all about. You see America was so busy with Sigmund Freud that they ignored Pavlov's teaching on conditioning (which was teaching by continually gratifying or punishing with each response). Shell Shock was the only term that our doctors understood at that time.

It wasn't until after the Korean War when our boys were so terribly brain-washed that they would recite communist teachings over and over. Some of our boys would just pull covers over their heads and die with no apparent illness at all. Our psychologists moved fast to get away from the sexually focused teaching of Freud to the conditioning theory of Pavlov. Doctors began to get an understanding of emotional breakdowns, and how to brainwash people. If you hear something often enough continually you will soon begin to believe it especially if a reward is given with it...no matter how outlandish it is.

It is being used today in "Global Warming". If something is said often enough people begin to believe it no matter how outrageous the idea might be. Then after a few years we change our opinion when we don't hear about it anymore. One doctor says eggs are bad for you. So everyone stops eating eggs. Then another doctor or report comes out and says that eggs are the best nourishment we can ever eat, so people start eating eggs again.

After more than a hundred years taking aspirins, people are told how bad they are for them and everyone stops taking aspirins, until another study appears, saying that you should take aspirins to stop strokes and heart attacks, then everyone is taking aspirins again. When will we as individuals under Gods authority stop allowing ourselves to be brainwashed and manipulated? Wake up world and smell the roses.

Meet the Eternal God, the World is managed by Him. We cannot make it rain when we want it to or make it stop raining at our discretion. Who do we think we are? God??

We don't realize as Americans how much we have been "brain washed". Look at the word Social. We have it in everything we say now like; social engineering, social studies, social worker, social justice, etc. All this does is brain wash us to accept the word for good and buy the acceptance of the word SOCIALISM, which used to be a dirty word to Americans, because it meant to us lose of freedom, and more government restrictions. It used to be History that we studied but now it is Social Studies.

Dad would read and reread the letters that his "Buddy" had sent him, and wondered where he was buried and what had happened. Had he died bravely? Had the accident been his fault? How many others were in the plane when it crashed?

Nobody else really knew the devastation that hit Dad at this time. He had visions of passing on to his son the real estate empire he had dreamed of, just as his father had passed his dreams on to him. Every day waking up he was reminded that Buddy was gone never to be seen again, never to be joked with and laughed with or cried with or hugged. He was gone. How final that thought was each morning. It would chew him up if he let it.

Dad felt his task was to find out how he died and what had happened to him in his last hours, so he wrote several contacts that he had met during his years as mayor, but to no avail. However, one of the kids in the Northwood neighborhood (who had gone to kindergarten with him, "Bud MacDonald"), wrote home to his Mother and shared the shock of the whole episode with her. Bud MacDonald was stationed over in England with Bud Clawson. He was also a pilot. His sister Dode was with the Red Cross, also in the same area. It really is a small world. Kids you had gone to grade school with were with you in the same area in England.

Northwood McDonald house on Houstonia.

The Letter he wrote home reads as follows:

February 24, 1944
Dear Mother:

It's been some time since last I wrote to you all. Lots have happened too. Really I should have written but sometimes it is impossible to do what you want to.

What I shall say now – you already know. This is the bad news first- Bud Clawson's co-pilot for awhile was Wise. During the Christmas maneuvers, he was returning from a pass in town when the truck he was riding in, left the road and struck the hedge row along the road which over turned the truck- Wise was pinned under the truck and crushed. He lived a few minutes but was unconscious until he died. Schultz was in that truck but came out with minor cuts.

Now you know that my boyhood friend is gone too. What caused his death I cannot say now, but I was there and saw it happen. Bud's ship crashed into the side of a hill and exploded. Both Bud and Dell Schultz were thrown clear, so that they did not burn with the ship. Both were killed instantly. There were eleven others on the ship. All died, in fact there was nothing left of the ship.

The remains of Bud's plane February 8, 1944.

The entire group felt the loss of these boys deeply. They were well known to all and liked and respected by all.

Tommie, Joe and I went to the funeral – A beautiful place in Southern England. Silver Taps – a volley of rifles three times sounding through the hills. Bud's squadron wheeling over head with an empty position in their double "V"- I shall never forget nor cease to long for my lost Buddy. A great little guy.

I feel the deepest sympathy for poor little Penny (Schultz) – They were such a fine pair – We know how she feels. God help them in their sorrow.

Dick Burr – the little boy from Flint - killed when we arrived in England. Wise, Bud, & Dell – All good friends of mine – All from Michigan. These things I have known for months yet I could not speak of them. It's been hard to keep my letters cheery.

Earl Metcalf who spent his last leave with Dode and I failed to return from his last mission, two days later.

Daddy always said, "Good soldiers don't cry" – Daddy was wrong.

Mamma! – Its nice to be a 1ˢᵗ Lt. And fly a big aeroplane – But I would "chuck" it all to be a little boy again and climb "in da middle" on Sunday morning and feel safe.

Not everything is so hard to take over here. Sometimes the roughness is smoothed out quite nice. I've just returned from a

*week in Northern Ireland. Touring Ireland with Jeep and Plane
is thrilling. – Put the Jeep in the ship and head for adventure. In
the part of the country where the Mourn Mountains meet the sea
– Emmmmm – You should see it. As beautiful as any any part of
the world that I have seen – Even as lovely as Scotland. Had quite
a nice time in Belfast and I would like to go back again sometime.
Stopped off at Glasgow for a day on the way back.*

Hope to see Dode for a few days soon.

Received your long letter of Jan 30, and V-mail 71.

*Thank you. Robin writes once a week now – quite
encouraging.*

*Everything goes fine here with me except that I miss you all so
very much. I shall write again this week.*

Love to all -   Your Bud.

*Lt. John A. MacDonald   0800375
77ʰ T.C.S. – 435 T.C.G.
A.P.O. #638 PM-N.Y.VC.*

Then, Mrs. MacDonald, received this letter from her daughter
Dode. I believe she was with the Red Cross.

Dearest mother _

*I wish there was something I could do to mitigate somewhat
the grief of Bud Clawson's family and Del's. Our Bud was here
all day yesterday and gave me complete details of the tragedy and
if it is any consolation for them to know that death came instantly,
they have it. I'm sure Bud has written all of this in his letter, but
I'll repeat it, just in case.*

*The group was on maneuvers – practicing supply drops - Bud's
plane being in the last formation. It is believed that one of the
supply boxes rammed the rear door, for it blew off and wrapped
itself around the tail, thus making it useless. The ship pulled out
of formation slowly and started downward. It's nose kept pulling
up, Bud doing all he could to bring her down safely. They hit the
top of the hill and exploded, but had they cleared the hill-top, they
might have landed safely, so that the boys had a chance and must*

have known it. Their realization of inescapable death must have been very brief indeed. The end came swiftly and suddenly.

The American Cemetery is at Brookwood, Guilford, near London – a most beautiful place of green lawns and stately trees. In my next letter I will send a picture, if I can, of the cemetery. One is not permitted to photograph temporary graves, but since all are marked alike with simple, white crosses, the graves in the picture will be exactly similar to others on the ground.

Our Bud said that the ceremony was very impressive. A formation of planes flew – overhead - five planes in a six-plane pattern. "Still together in spirit"! Bud's position being vacant.

Please express to the two families my sympathy my very deep sympathy. They were very fine boys – with gay hearts and great courage; an inspiration now to all their friends.

All my love,
Dode.

In the next few months others wrote of what they saw and how it all came about.

March 25, 1944
Dear Sir:

Almost a month ago I wrote to you and Mrs. C telling you the details of the crash. Recently my family tells me that some of my mail doesn't seem to be coming through, and when it does, it's usually late. With this thought in mind I'll try to repeat most of that letter now.

A large formation of our ships was flying a practice mission dealing with resupply of equipment from the air. My ship had been converted into a photographic ship and was being used for motion picture shots of the mission. I was flying outside the formation and about as near to Bud as anyone in the sky that day. I was told I could fly any place relative to the formation, so naturally I took up a position close to my pals so that they would appear in the pictures. This was my position at the time of the crash.

We had dropped our supplies and were continuing in flight

when Bud's ship suddenly dived down to the left and under me. I saw him pull the ship back once to level flight then another dive as he passed under my ship. Turning quickly I circled the ship which had burst into flame immediately on contact with the ground. Bud had been riding pilot and Schultz co-pilot. The altitude was such that it was impossible to use chutes. Three crew members were thrown clear; Bud, Shultz, and the radio operator. Death was instantaneous.

I was the first man from our squadron to reach the scene, and together with Capt. C.A.Erb (a very good friend of Bud and Schultz) accompanied the bodies to the hospital.

As we drove up to the accident we had seen three ambulances several medical men and fire fighting equipment already there. At the hospital positive identity was established, personal property removed and services arranged for Feb. 10th at Brookwood Cemetery. The cemetery is quite large and a very beautiful part has been set aside for use of the United Nations. There is a permanent section begun in the last war, and the temporary part now in use. This entire section is in the form of a park and very pretty.

On Feb. 10th our squadron paid last respects to the crew of "052". While most of our personnel attended services at the graves, a formation of ships circled above There was one space left open in the formation, the one usually occupied by Bud and Schultz. A fitting tribute to good fliers.

Will you please accept my sincere sympathy for the sorrow in your home. I believe I know how much you were counting on him to return home; especially you Mr. C. But I can't help but feel what an ideal way this was to leave all of you. Many of us once here realize we may never come home, and I can think of no better ending for a job than to quit it while doing that part you like best. I shall be very glad to answer any questions of any type and hope to be able to enclose photographs the next time I write.

Sincerely,

Elmo

Lt. E.W. Frome   0-799371
75 T.C. Sqdn. A.P.O. 638
c/oP.M. N.Y.C.

My Dad had to reply to Elmo's letter immediately.

Dear Elmo:

In reply to your letter of March 25th, I want to say that I was more than pleased to hear from you. It was certainly kind of you to write. I did not receive your letter you mentioned as having sent a month prior to this one, in which you gave the details of Bud's death. We have at no time had any information as to the cause of Bud's death, and it has been extremely hard for me to take. Bud was the only boy and I had built up high ideas for him after he had his job for his country, and of course it will take time to really get back to normal. Bud's mother has taken his death very hard. It is natural that a Mother would. It will probably take her some time to get out of her blue mood.

I have heard from the well known grapevine a few of the instances that happened, one I believe you might be able to advise me of its truth. It seems he was flying and the door of his plane blew off and lodged in his wing, which either changed the air directions or locked the wings so that it could not be operated by anybody. Also, I believe there were more of the boys in the plane than the mere five men of the crew. The motion pictures you took of the mission might reveal some of these details.

Bud sent me a picture of his crew taken just a few days before he was killed, and it showed a great deal of change in Bud's face. I always remember and knew him as a happy go lucky boy. I had always tried to teach him to make and keep everybody as a friend, and I believe he did that. We have had so many nice letters from everybody all over, and I know of no one who would say or think differently. You mentioned that Capt. Erb accompanied the bodies to the hospital. Bud spoke of him very highly. He said he was a swell guy and liked him very much.

I am very glad you told me about the place where Bud was buried, about his funeral and the services held at the cemetery. All I can say is that he did his best and gave everything he had, and I am glad they gave him such a fine tribute as I always thought he was an exceptionally good flyer. I presume that his personal belongings will come to us at some later date. I wish you would write me as to the truth of the grapevine stories I mentioned above, because it would make it clear in my mind that it was utterly impossible for any human being to overcome this accident which was caused by something beyond his control. Bud MacDonald wrote his Mother a letter after the accident. It was a very nice letter, and Mrs. MacDonald let me read it, which I appreciated very much, As you know, Bud went to school with him, in fact they started in the Kindergarten together at home.

Now for the other side of life, Margie and TC are both having their usual good time. I think you remember both of them. TC was the Younger and always wanted to do things that sometimes others didn't want to do, such as going to a show when we wanted to bowl. Margie has become a hostess in the Officer's Club here in Detroit, which has its headquarters in the Tuller Hotel, which is a very nice place for it, and I think the Officers all enjoy it very much. It seems they have more hostesses than they can use so they take turns and nights through the week. Margie seems to draw Saturday night or Sunday assignments, which is when most of the boys are there. So if you ever get to Detroit, maybe Margie can help you get acquainted.

I am always interested in your work, so if you get the time, drop me a line, although I suppose you have quite a bit of letter writing to do, which keeps you quite busy, but in case you have a few spare moments let me know something about you and your work. If there is anything I can do for you or anything you would like, don't hesitate to mention it as I would be only to glad to do anything in my power for you.

Again I want to thank you very much for your thoughtfulness in writing me, and maybe you can clear up the entire picture in my mind as to Bud and I certainly would like the photographs you mentioned if you are able to send them.

Sincerely Yours,
Bud's Dad

Another letter that came in April was from his flight commander.
April 2, 1944

Dear Mr. and Mrs. Clawson,

I'd like to introduce myself to you first of all. I'm Captain E. A. Smith, Flight Commander of B Flight, 75th T.C.Sqdn. My friends call me Larry, and so did Bud, who was one of my very best friends. Lloyd, or Bud, was in B. Flight. We think it was the best flight of the best squadron in the Troop Carrier Command, and Bud was as good a formation flyer as anyone I've ever seen.

He was as you know rather mischievous, always doing something, and he seemed to get around to a great many things always. Perhaps that is why he was good in the air he also tried to learn all he could, and altho he sometimes put himself in precarious positions, he always came out all right. The experience he gained during these times made him probably the one most nearly capable of getting out of a jam of all pilots. I'd have bet on him. Bud was good.

On this mission Bud was flying on my left wing. With his regular combat crew. Schultz, Frith, Machowiak, and Barth. Lt. Schultz was his co-pilot, a very likable lad. Lt. Firth was his navigator, and quite proficient. Sgt. Barth was the crew chief and Sgt. Machowiak, the radio Operator.

From Top left to right: Lt. Firth, the navigator, Lt. Bud Clawson,
Lt. Schultz. Bottom row from left to right: Sgt. Machowiak,
the radio operator, Sgt. Barth, crew chief.

We had huge bundles in the cabin of our ships, all attached to parachutes, to be pushed out of the main cabin door, for supplying troops on the ground.

As we flew over the dropping area the bundles began to go out, but one apparently pushed the cargo door off the hinges. The door forced itself into his horizontal stabilizer (the tail) and left him with almost no control over the up and down movement of the ship. He dropped out of formation as the nose fell and even got the ship to fly level for a few seconds, but without the control surfaces he could not keep it up, and the ship struck the ground.

Lloyd was laid to rest with his crew in the American Cemetery at Brookwood, near London, during which a formation of his buddies flew over as taps was sounded. Lloyd was nicknamed "The Duke", and we always called him that. He has been sent two or three packages containing cookies and candy, which we have given to his friends, and the photography equipment and film is being returned to you thru military channels with his effects.

These messages to you are not supposed to be written until we hear from you that the War Dept. has notified you, but we have heard from parents of some of his crew and therefore believe this message is now in order.

He was a swell fellow! I counted him as one of my best friends and had hoped to meet you all after the war. If circumstances permit I'd still like to someday.

With my sincerest regrets,
Capt. Larry Smith

Captain Larry Smith 0-729254
75ᵗʰ Troop Carrier Squadron
435ᵗʰ Troop Carrier Gp.
A.P.O. #133, c/o Postmaster
New York City, New York

Another immediate reply came from Dad.

Dear Larry,
I certainly appreciated very much your kind letter of April 2ⁿᵈ, in which you gave me details and cleared up my mind as to the cause of my son, Bud's

death. Bud was my only son and it seems extremely hard to believe that I will never see him again. I had built up many hopes and had planned on his helping me in the future. Bud's Mother has taken his death very hard, naturally the Mother seems to have a more difficult job overcoming the shock than anyone else. We are fortunate to have two daughters left, which is different than some parents who lose their only child. I certainly can sympathize with them in every respect.

We received official notice of his on the 16th of February, the accident happened, as you know, on the 8th of February. I always felt and knew that he would give the best he had in him, in fact he has given all. In one of his letters, he enclosed a picture of him and his group, which he called "the best group in the best squadron in the troop Transport Command". Bud was always a happy go lucky lad all through his life and always had a lot of friends, but I guess no one can get around such accidents as that which caused his death. I have received several letters from other buddies of his, but your letter is the first one giving the details of the accident, and I want to thank you very much for this information as it clears up everything in my mind. I certainly hope that none of the other boys will have misfortune of this type.

I am very glad that you will be able to send back his personal belongings and his photographic equipment. We have taken pictures of Bud and the rest of the family from infancy up. I am very happy to hear that the candies, cookies and other edibles were given to the other boys, and I certainly hope they enjoyed them. Some day I want to go to England and see the place of burial and make arrangements at that time for his return home so that he can be buried here, which I know can't be done until after the war.

I want very much to meet you and become acquainted with you after the war is over. I wish you would let me know your home address so that we can get together and probably you will be able to tell me more about Bud and his work at that time.

Again I want to thank you for all you have told me and for your very kind letter and for taking care of Bud's things for us. Please let us know if there is anything I can get for you here in this country, as I would be only to glad to send you anything you might want.

I remain
Sincerely yours,
H.Lloyd Clawson   (Bud's Dad)

Then a year later a letter from CAPTAIN Edward W. Frome, (Elmo,) arrived.

Dear Mr. & Mrs. C.
February 12, 1945

Meant this to be written on the 8ᵗʰ of this month but I've been away from home, at a base where the facilities are very limited. I believe that you will understand and realize the circumstances.

Top row middle soldier is Ed (Elmo) Frome.

Maj. Larry Smith, Capt Erb and my fellow members of "B" Flight(that to which "The Duke" belonged) join me in extending our sincere sympathies to you and your family at this time. I am sure we'll remember the 1ˢᵗ part of Feb. 1944 and especially what it will always mean to you.

Should you be interested in what we have been doing, our activities would read something like this. June of last year (1944) saw us engage in the Normandy invasion, and August saw us taking part in the landing in S. France. We returned to England and we took part in the invasion of Holland and the doings at Bastogne. Between invasions we've been hauling freight and evacuating wounded from front and rear areas. While stationed in Italy awaiting the invasion of S. France, we had ample time to see Rome and since our return to U.K. have seen Paris often. Have yet to see Berlin but we're not in any hurry for this latter trip unless the Russians get there first.

Our group has been given the Unit Citation for action in Normandy while all combat personnel have been given the Air Medal for Normandy and clusters to this award for S. France and Holland. From our work with Airborne Troops, we've gotten to know some of them very well. When called on to work for them at Bastogne we were especially anxious to help and felt mighty fine when they gave us credit for doing a good job. To me this was our best job so far.

That's about all of interest from here. Would like to hear from you and what is happening at home. Should you see "Penny" Schultz or correspond with her please send our regards.

Sincerely yours,
Ed Frome

Later Eddy said to me, "I personally took the wallet from his pocket and the wings off his shirt. The wallet I gave to our commanding officer. The wings I wore on my flying clothes the rest of the war. The same wings I gave to your Dad the first time I came to see your family in Royal Oak".

Chapter 5
Over Coming Our Problems

The rest of the war seemed to me to drag on and on. We were a very unhappy family. Mom didn't want to live and was hospitalized for a period of time. How do you know what to say to someone who doesn't want to live. I was a teenager and I felt lonely and every bone in my body ached with anguishing pain. I would so love to sooth my Mom and Dad, and step back in time to make life as it was before our tragedy, but I couldn't do anything for them. There were so many hurting people here in the USA. It was a difficult time for everyone.

Life would never be as it once was again, and I knew we had to put one foot in front of the other and go on, no matter how hard it was. People often said that time would heal the pains that we all were experiencing, but it certainly didn't seem that way to us then.

As my Mom lay on the hospital bed, I felt that I wanted to crawl up on the bed with her, so I did just that. I hugged her and started crying, and telling her that I still needed her too. She and I hugged each other and cried sobbing, in each other's arms, while Dad stood back and watched. Later I realized that he was hurting too, but just seeing us and realizing how much we needed each other: was healing for him.

Time went on more rapidly after that, but I couldn't practice my saxophone lessons in the basement anymore. It made my mother feel too sad, so I went over to Dad's office on Woodward Ave. across from the Shrine. I practiced there before anyone got to the office. I was still taking lessons from Larry Teal, who played with the Detroit Symphony. I so appreciated him as a teacher. He was so kind to me, though we both knew I would never be a great saxophone player.

The office across from the Shrine on Woodward.

I wanted to "challenge" Bill Muncy for the first saxophone chair and Mr. Denman our band director, urged me on, so I learned to play a very fast piece, called "Piggly-Wiggle" by Edward Barrol, silly name but a light hearted melody. Bill was better than I was, and of course he knew it. He was a cocky kid, and you couldn't help but like him. He was sure of himself, which was a quality the rest of us did not have. I heard Bill was killed in a boating accident years later.

At this time "Olie" Green, had a group of our Royal Oak band members in a combo he called, "Olie and the Nasty Nose Pickers". Oliver went on to play with the Detroit Symphony for many years. He is related to the Starr family here in Royal Oak. Victor Barrett played Trombone, Don DeWolf, played Clarinet, Chick Webb played clarinet , Oliver green played clarinet, and Howard Emery played trumpet. The fellow on the far left of the photograph could be Jim Geister or Bill Muncy. Bill played Alto Sax and Jim played tenor and this fellow has a baritone sax. Oh well, that's the way it goes when people don't put names on their photo's.

Ollie Green and "The Nasty Nose Pickers". left to right: Bill Muncey
or Jim Geister next to Victor Barrett who played trombone, Don
DeWolf played clarinet, Chick Webb played Clarinet, Oliver
Green played clarinet and Howard Emery played trumpet.

During this time my Dad spoke to many, many, people about the
hospital that he wanted for Royal Oak. Even when I was playing golf
with Don DeWolf and his father, my father was praising the work of the
Hospital Authority in Royal Oak, and was also soliciting funds. Most
of the early money that came into Beaumont's bank account came from
Dad's buddies at Red Run Golf Club.

During the War we had a hard time finding new golf balls, so we
used our old ones. Rubber was scarce and the golf balls had a lot of
rubber in them. The balls at that time split apart and you could easily
put a smile on them if you hit your shot incorrectly. We really worked
hard at hitting the perfect shot. Most all my balls had "smiles" all over
them.

My teenage years were very difficult with the War, and the death
of my only brother. They were painful years that I tried hard to ignore
as time went on, but as I write these memories I see how unnatural life
was back then. We went from the Great Depression to the World War
that was to be the "end of all Wars". Ha Ha.! Only fools believe they
can stop wars.

Only when the Messiah (not President Obama) comes again will wars actually stop. Bullies will always have to be put in their place. They just keep coming up at us in different ways and good people have to counter act their attacks in new and different ways.

We were struggling as a family. We all loved one another, but at this time living was as if each of us had a deep hole inside. Before the war we were united as a family, but after the tragedy of Bud's death, we were a family that had a missing spot in all our lives. Through no action of our own, our lives were changed. Overnight a horrible nightmare happened. People who have tragic accidents happen to them know what I mean. We once were an entire family with each of us having our own flaws, but now we each had pain added to our problems.

My senior year at Royal Oak High School was the most tumultuous time in my life. I had been asking my Dad for four years if I could go to Kingswood School, the girl's school of Cranbrook, because my brother and my sister had attended school there. He finally said yes my senior year. Like most of the schools I had experienced in my life time, they had to prove they were superior (and they probably were). However, I was not prepared to make a transition my senior year, I should have done it four years before. They felt that I was not well enough prepared to go to college and wanted me to go back a year in school, which I did agree to do.

After awhile though I felt that I had made a mistake when my friends Barbara Baldwin, Malcolm Jamieson, Bill Rauchle, Jeanne Johnson and Suzanne Boone, would all be graduating that June. I asked my folks if I could go back to Royal Oak High School, so happily I found myself back. I was short one class necessary for graduation, which I was relieved to know I could make it up in summer school. The school said that they would send me my diploma after the class was completed.

Usually the graduating classes had a special outing and the classes before ours would always go to Washington D.C. to be taken on a grand tour of our Capital, but our class did not because of the War. We had to stay local, so we chose to go to Bob-Lo, an amusement park island between Detroit and Canada. Oh, the excitement we all felt to go by boat, to a special place to eat and dance and ride the amusement rides. It was so thrilling just to think about it in the weeks before it ever happened.

The big day came and my sister came along with me and my friends.

It was really a short boat ride, but a tremendous storm came up and we had no way of knowing what was going to happen. The captain of the ship found himself in a terrible situation. He could not dock at Bob-lo nor could he go back and dock in Detroit's harbor, so we "rode" the storm out at sea. My memory of the event was seeing the teachers and the students leaning over the railings losing all their food and there was no food to buy or eat. A few of us sat in the middle of the top deck and played cards until we finally docked at about 11pm that night. We went right home, and I don't know what the others did. I heard some of the boys stopped at a bar on the way home and had a few beers.

Shortly after that the War ended and we could start living a normal life again.

Chapter 6
Learning to Live with a Hole in Your Life

I called my golfing friend Barbara Ellis and we rode the Woodward Avenue bus into the heart of Detroit to celebrate with all the other folks who were cheering that the Big War was over. It was 1945 and I had graduated from High School at Royal Oak High that summer. We knew it wouldn't be long before Japan would fall. Everyone was kissing and hugging everyone else. I had never before seen such exuberance. Life Magazine had a picture that became famous, a sailor kissing a nurse in the middle of the street of New York. We had people out playing their trumpets, and violinists, out playing their fiddles. We were ecstatic. We were expressing our joy any way we knew how: Dancing, jumping, shouting, and drinking. A big load had been lifted off our backs! My friend and I didn't drink but just to be with all the Americans rejoicing was good enough for us. We rode the Woodward bus to Detroit and home from the celebration.

A few months later Dad received a call from Elmo. He was considering being discharged and had a chance to see us before he settled down in Maryland. It was so wonderful seeing him again.

Captain Ed Frome and Lloyd Clawson out to eat at the Bowery.

We were all curious as to what he was planning to do now that the war was over. He had been raised by his mother and aunt when his father had passed away and they had done a marvelous job raising him for he was a fine gentleman. After looking back over all the years of my life, I can honestly say he was a wonderful replacement for the beloved son and brother we had lost. My brother would have been a wonderful man had life dealt him a different hand. Eddie a positive person was so kind. He would give us a sweet answer or a little laugh or chuckle and then an answer to whatever circumstance that came up.

Eddie surely was a gift from God in our lives. He might not have ever known it but we did. We needed him. He became my big brother who had all the answers when I needed them. He was a wonderful buddy to my Dad and my Mom. We were able to pull ourselves up out of the misery the war had left us in and into the light of American Freedom, in the land we loved. He had a wonderful gift of always seeing life as positive, a glass ½ full not ½ empty.

Soon Eddy went back home to the girl he married 10 days after getting home from overseas and married. Dorothy was so sweet and so adorable. At first glance you could see why he loved her. She didn't have a "mean bone in her body". She was a sweet, sweet pretty little girl who adored "Elmo".

Left to right: Bill Michell, Cheryl Michell, Lloyd Clawson, Little Annette Michell, Val Clawson, Roy Michell, Barbara Frome, Dorothy Frome and David Frome, Circa 1963.

At one point they moved into the little building that later became the office of Kirk Mills, a builder for Dad. (He built the house we live in today). The little building was near the auditorium and the tennis courts and had been used for various shops throughout and before the war years.

They had two children Barbara and David, who after they graduated wanted to move to Arizona, thus the whole family moved there too. Eddy had given us his healing touch. He would always be my brother. He had made our life meaningful again.

Eddie and Bud 1943.

Chapter 7
Wm. Beaumont Hospital

Lloyd Clawson had dug in his heels and pushed harder for a big new hospital in Royal Oak. He knew that a city with a successful business would bring a lot of extra money from visitors. For awhile they thought that it might move to Birmingham, but Lloyd Clawson had secured a lot more land than Birmingham and the decision was made for Royal Oak to be the location in Oakland County. Lloyd had talked many hours with Dr Rudemann at Ford Hospital (his eye doctor) about how locked in the Ford Hospital was because they had no more land. There were houses all tightly packed around them, and no place to grow.

The big project then was to choose a name for the planned hospital. For various reasons the names they chose did not work. Finally they asked if he would give $10,000 more to the Board, if so they would name it after him. It would be called the H. Lloyd Clawson Hospital, but he turned it down not because of the money, but because he was too humble a man to have it named after him. Shortly after that someone came up with the name of "William Beaumont", a perfect name because he was a famous French doctor from Michigan, who discovered stomach acids.

After the War was over and life began to get back to normal, Dad decided to take the Detroit Board of Commerce International Trade Tour. He was selected as one of the 45 Detroit business men to study industry and trade conditions in Europe and Great Britain. The World Affairs Committee was under the auspices of the Detroit Board of Commerce. On the tour their first stop was Milan, Italy where they conferred with the city's business and industrial leaders and inspected the trade fair. This was an 18 day flying trip.

Dad went on several of these trips all over the world. I have a picture taken when he was in Taiwan talking to Chiang Kai-Shek and another when he had mounted a camel in Egypt. The Tribune Newspaper said of Lloyd Clawson, long active in Royal Oak affairs both civic and political, is president of the Realty Service Company, said this,

Claire Booth Luce welcoming the Detroit Board of Commerce.

Lloyd talking to Chiang Kai-shek.

"Naturally, as a real estate man, I will be particularly interested in the post-war real estate development and rebuilding programs in these war-torn countries. Our group is composed of men from all walks of life, and our purpose is to see what can be done to stimulate trade as well as familiarize ourselves with conditions abroad. I am very happy to take part in this project which is certainly an opportunity that does not come along every day".

Lloyd and Val at Chamber of Commerce 1955.

In 1955 he was awarded the Chamber of Commerce Outstanding Citizen Award and received a wonderful letter from his friend George Dondero. It read as follows:

GEORGE A. DONDERO
18TH DISTRICT, MICHIGAN

HOME ADDRESS:
ROYAL OAK, MICH.

SECRETARIES:
LUCIE A. FORD
ELIZABETH A. MUOLLO
ROSE M. SANKO

COMMITTEE ON PUBLIC WORKS

WASHINGTON ADDRESS:
1414 HOUSE OFFICE BUILDING

Congress of the United States
House of Representatives
Washington, D. C.

May 2, 1955

Mr. Lloyd Clawson
2135 Northwood
Royal Oak, Michigan

Dear Lloyd:

It was with considerable personal grati-
fication that I read of the recognition extended
to you by the people of our home city of Royal Oak.

I know of no one in our midst more deserv-
ing of the honor conferred upon you than yourself.
Through the years, and I am in a position to say
this perhaps as forcefully as any man living in our
area, you have been a fine civic leader, a generous
citizen, and an incessant worker for the good of
the city we call home.

I congratulate you, and join with the many
citizens of Royal Oak in the satisfaction that comes
to us all for recognizing one who has earned it with
his goodness to our people.

Your old admiring friend,

George A. Dondero, M. C.

GAD/s

97

School District of the City of Royal Oak

ROYAL OAK, MICHIGAN
May 2, 1955

Office of N. J. QUICKSTAD
Director of Special Services

Mr. Lloyd Clawson
2135 Northwood Blvd.
Royal Oak, Michigan

Dear Lloyd:

Although this note is belated, it is nevertheless sincere
and I am very happy that you were selected The Man of The
Year by the Chamber of Commerce.

You have done much for this community, and I,personally,
have appreciated the help that you gave me in my early
days of administrative work in Royal Oak.

I trust that your many deeds of service will be a source
of great comfort to you. God bless you!

Sincerely,

Nat-

Lloyd and my Mom, Val, would often go on trips to Alaska or to Mexico with his old friend Clyde Lawson and Grace his wife, to the Rockies. They went where ever they fancied in their later years. He began to leave more of his work up to Eddy Frome and Art Laurie, Clyde's son-in-law. At one point they needed to name a new street in back of Vinsetta so Dad suggested they name it after both of them and they came up with Laurome. Eddy told me of how my street Vinsetta got its name from Bassett and Vinton. Many of Northwood's streets are named after residents whom lived here at the time; Smith, Galpin, Lyons to name a few.

Art Laurie and Bud 1943.

As time went on Dad lost his eyesight because of diabetes, glucoma, or both I'm not sure which, but he had had diabetes since he was about 40 years old. However, he continued to go to the Wm. Beaumont Board meeting with the help of Hugh Heagerty, his loyal employee and dear friend.

He was a very generous man who gave land to the Congregational Church, Royal Oak city land for the fire station on Webster to Royal Oak, and land for the Northwood School to the school board on which he served for two terms. During the Great Depression years, he also took all the children from Northwood School to the Shrine Circus by chartered buses, for he was a thirty-second degree Mason and believed in supporting their activities. He also chartered buses to take children from all the Royal Oak schools at different times to the Children's Concerts, at Orchestra Hall, narrated by Edith Rhetts. He loved Royal Oak and the people of Royal Oak loved him.

I'll add a final touch to my story about Eddy Frome jokingly called "Elmo" by my brother and their other war friends. When I went out to Arizona with my husband Jim, we met up with Eddy and Dorothy. They showed us the Grand Canyon sundown and sunrise. Eddy took me aside and told me something that I had never heard before. He explained what transpired that fatal day on February 8th, 1944. Bud had been assigned to take the photographers out in the mock war practice that demonstration day. Eddy very much wanted to do it, so Bud let him take the assignment and Buddy took Eddy's place in formation.

I don't believe things happen by accident. God knows all things from the beginning to the end. We don't and we jump to conclusions that God allowed this bad thing. It is my opinion that there is a devil who is trying to destroy everyone he can, and I see a God who wants to give us life and life "more abundantly". God knew we needed to achieve His purposes, so He brought this wonderful young American man into our family's life to fill the hole made by Bud's death. One that the devil had created, and in doing this made it possible for us to carry out God's wishes for our lives.

On July 16th, 1971, Lloyd Clawson lost his fight for life. The pain of his son's death and his own blindness were no longer his concern. He had fulfilled all of the goals that he had set his heart on. He had left Royal Oak a better place. Beaumont Hospital was succeeding as he had planned, and it would continue helping his beloved city succeed during the hard times that might follow. His Grandson William Roy Michell, gave the grave side eulogy and Father Coughlin gave his eulogy at Wm. Sullivans Funeral home in Royal Oak. Dad had preserved the land near the Shrine that was used for parking, his office on Woodward and his home on Northwood Blvd. When he retired he offered to sell all the land to Father Coughlin for $85,000.

Office sold to Shrine.

They had been good friends for many, many years, and Dad had never wanted to sell that land to anyone else, others had tried to buy it many times before but he knew in his heart that Father should have it.

A Memorial resolution was given to the Clawson family from the South Oakland Hospital Authority:

"With profound sorrow and sincere appreciation for his many contributions to the South Oakland Hospital Authority, the members of the Authority, hereby set forth upon the permanent record our great sense of loss over the passing, on July 16, 1971, of our fellow member and friend H. Lloyd Clawson

Mr. Clawson was a member of the South Oakland Hospital Authority from the beginning, serving continuously until the time of his death. He was active in the conception and planning of both the Authority and William Beaumont Hospital.

Mr. Clawson always exerted a significant and constructive influence on our services to the community. He was a faithful and willing worker. Ready always to respond to the hospitals needs.

Mr. Clawson's death is a great loss to all of us who worked with him over the many years of his devoted service to the South Oakland Hospital Authority. The benefit of his wise counsel and broad experience in public endeavors will be sorely missed.

It is, therefore, with profound sorrow and deep appreciation that we unanimously adopt this memorial resolution for H. Lloyd Clawson".

All this tribute was to a man who tried to keep everyone happy. He was a "little guy" with a happy walk and a "stogie cigar" always in his mouth. In my entire life I never heard him say a bad thing about anyone except my Mom and that was when he was angry at her, then he would call her "the old Battle-Axe" which always made us laugh, even my Mom. Neither of my parents ever swore, so these Hollywood movies that depict elderly people as cursing were wrong. Many older Americans were good ….. just that ….. GOOD!

End of Book 2

TRILOGY THREE

BOOK THREE
The Vilified Priest

Memories of the "Greatest Generation" and of the Roman Catholic Priest who helped to shape them:

Father Charles E Coughlin

By TC Christman

Many people have encouraged me to write my memories of Father Charles E Coughlin. I have included some of these in my book, "The Dream Cruise", however, there were many more stories that my family and I experienced, because we were personally involved. He has been vilified by a lot of Jewish people because of his hatred for communism which was started by atheistic Jewish people. He could not understand how a group of people who called themselves Jews could denounce the God of Abraham, Isaac and Jacob, and become atheists.

Starting a foundation for the Shrine school. From left to right: 1st person is lawyer Fletch Renton, later a judge, Father Coughlin dedicating their new school.

Before all of the talk of communism, one of those heart felt remembrances began in the 1930's when Father Coughlin decided to get a Great Dane for a pet. We all admired this huge pup, whose name was "Pal", but this big puppy turned out to be more of a trickster than Father expected. One evening he broke loose and started to patrol the area. What joy! He discovered a whole nest of rabbits all together, just waiting for him. So he commenced to eradicate their box, the wire and all else that got in his way, also annihilating the hapless inhabitants.

The next morning the little boy who owned them, came out to take care of his beloved rabbits only to find them all gone and the box parts scattered all over the back yard. He looked from one end to the other to locate at least one of his bunnies, but alas all had disappeared. Soon it was discovered that the culprit who pulled off this caper was none other than "Pal", Fathers new puppy. Needless to say, Father felt terrible about the incident and looked long and hard for a solution to repay the lad for such a great loss.

Leonard Hebel on 727 Gardenia Avenue in Royal Oak had a nice livery stable and had recently acquired a Shetland pony for $10.00 from his former owner. It seemed the pony did not like living with the previous owner so he would break loose and wander around town. The police notified the owner to stable him properly or sell him, and he decided to sell the pony. Father Coughlin found out about the incident and bought "Ned" the pony, to placate the rabbit owner for Pal's, bad behavior. And that little boy was "Buddy" Clawson, my big brother.

What joy filled that young lad's life! He no longer mourned for his family of bunnies, now that he had a manlier creature to take care of, a horse of his own! However, it wasn't too long before the mischievous "Ned" got loose and started his old antics of wandering. Bud was frantic because his beloved pony was nowhere to be found.

1932 TC on Ned and Bud and Johnny Lyons in wagon.

A telephone call came to Bud's Dad. "Ned" had not run away, he had gone back to the livery stable where Father had gotten him, Leonard Hebel's Stable. Someone at the local newspaper heard of the story and printed it in the paper as an interesting local happening.

To stay with the story of Father's gift to Bud in June of 1931, a newspaper head line story title says, "1931, Mayor's Son Enters Parade". The article reads, "Ned, a 14 year old Shetland pony, is the first entry in the 'Doll and Pet Parade' to take place in Pontiac, Friday August 28. "Ned is owned by Lloyd "Buddy" Clawson, 13 year old son of Mayor H. Lloyd Clawson of Royal Oak. He was presented to Buddy last June, by Rev. Charles E. Coughlin Priest of the Shrine of the Little Flower". Buddy said, "I know a lot of boys who want to enter other ponies too. Believe me 'Ned's some pony! He's been places I've never been myself, one of those being in jail. A Policeman caught him walking around town late one night and put him in a cell. I guess Mr. Coughlin was surprised when he heard about that. Ned doesn't know it, but a man sold him for $10.00 one time. He doesn't look like a $10.00 horse now, does he? And he'll look better yet when I bring him to Pontiac".

Bud on Ned.

"The Daily Tribune is offering $100 in prizes to the boys and girls of Oakland County for the best entry in the event".

Ned was a member of our family for several more years and he stopped his wandering. I even had the privilege of riding him. He was stabled in Fred Galpins barn across from the Clawson sisters' house on Clawson Avenue. That old barn held a lot of memories for me.

The Clawson sisters house on Clawson Ave. in Royal Oak.

Chapter 2
Memories of My Early Spiritual Life

In referring to Father Coughlin's influence in our lives I will try and go chronologically if it is at all possible.

The first memory I have of him was when we were all waiting for him to come over and I thought of him as my Father not my Daddy. I loved and played with my Daddy all the time, but when Father came over he would talk to me and hold me.

Northwood DUR stop at Twelve Mile.

My parents hired a young girl to help my mother take care of me. Her name was Gretchen. She would prepare breakfast for us. The priests who were at the church or visiting the church had no place to go for breakfast, so for a time they came over to our house. Every now and then Father Coughlin would come too. My Mom was never around. In fact I don't remember my Mom ever getting up before eleven A.M., except when she had a golf engagement. As a kid, I tried to sleep in late but that just gave me a terrible headache.

I was about 2 or 3, one time when Father Coughlin came over, and when he did, I ran and jumped into his arms and he lifted me up and held me. I never forgot this because my sister yelled at me and told me I was never to do that again. I never did.

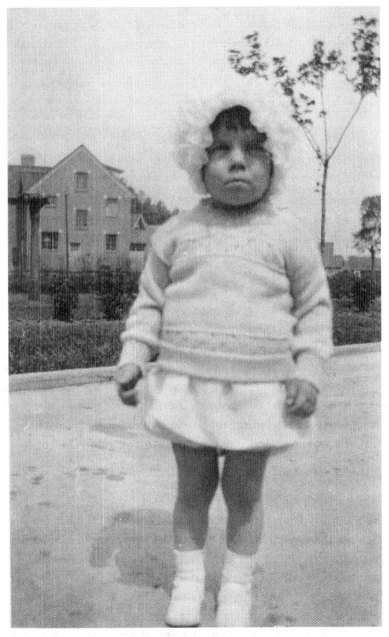

TC at 3 years old 1930.

In 1932 I started kindergarten at Northwood School with my

girl friends, Marian McCann, Jeanne Johnson and Barbara Baldwin. Malcolm Jamieson and Bill Rauchle were the two boys in our gang. In 1933, Marian and I were the only ones who went to the Shrine of the Little Flower Grade School. The others went to Northwood School. This provided me with a back ground education that has stayed with me all of my life.

Jeannie Johnson was used in a lot of pictures for subdivision.

The custom of the Catholic school was to have religion classes, taught by the nuns. They would tell stories of miracles that took place around or about children, or they would tell of miracles that took place with saints. I would never have gotten this teaching from the public school. Even though, the public schools in those days quite freely taught of Jesus (or even miracles) depending on who was teaching. At the Shrine school, religion was taught every day, and we went to Mass every morning.

I'm not too sure of the year this happened, but I think it was Sister Louise who began telling us about the devil. She told us how as little children we all believed in God and His son Jesus Christ, but when we grew up the devil would try and steal Him away from us. I remember gritting my teeth and saying to myself, "I won't let him do that to me". I imagined every child in the class did the same thing.

Sometime later I was going to throw some waste paper out in the trash can in the kitchen of our house, and I heard my Dad say, "I'm no atheist you are," to my Mom. I stopped and asked my Dad what an atheist was, and his reply was someone who doesn't believe in God. The thought came to me that perhaps I didn't have to believe in God.

In my little child's thinking I visualized an angel on my right shoulder and a devil on my left shoulder such as in the cartoons I saw at the movies. Then I remembered what Sister Louise taught us and I said, "I believe!"!

The Lord showed me, at that point, that He would never leave me or forsake me, and if you will, I became "Born Again" as the Gospel of John says one must be. I always thought that expression originated with extremely religious people until I found it for myself in St. John's gospel. Jesus said it, in the 3rd Chapter and the 3rd Verse. "I tell you a truth, unless a man is born again, he cannot SEE the kingdom of God". and in verse 5, "Verily, verily, I say unto you, Except a man, be born of water and of the Spirit, he cannot ENTER into the kingdom of God. That which is born of the flesh is flesh; and that which is born of the Spirit is spirit".

This is a real phenomenon that a person actually feels. I wish more people understood this experience. St. Paul says it this way, "Christ IN ME the hope of glory". The only way you can have this happen to you is to sincerely open your heart to Him and invite Him into your life. What a wonderful, tremendous feeling you will experience! Jesus says in Revelations, "I stand at the door and knock and if any man hears my voice and opens the door I will come in and sup with him and he with me". The door is your heart and the knob is inside your heart and YOU have to open that door.

One of my problems I had was that I was very rough. It was probably because I had an older sister and brother and they played that way with me. One of the nuns whose name was sister Francetta, was my favorite. She was very small, and very beautiful, and soft-spoken. On one occasion her beads caught in my notebook and when I tried to extract the book from the beads, I broke her rosary. I felt terrible. I knew it was because I was so rough. She was so sweet to me and said that I must not worry about it, and that she would fix it. She did with a bright red string. Every time I saw that red string I shuddered, and reminded myself to watch what I was doing.

In 1935 my Mom made the decision to leave the Roman Catholic Church. There was a time when my Mom became so upset with Father Coughlin getting involved with the politics of the time that she finally left the Church. Father felt badly that this happened, but he always believed that she would come back. I had gone to the Shrine's school in 1933, 1934, and 1935.

I decided in my heart to learn all I could in my religion class because I knew I probably would not go to the Church across the street anymore, so when Sister Louise started teaching us how much God wanted us to turn our problems over to Him on the altar of Grace, "I ate it up". I was to take my nail biting and give it to Him on His altar in the sky. I was thrilled to believe it would go away and it was months before I realized it was gone. Then I had another problem that I had to get rid of, that was a nervous tic I had picked up, of grabbing my chin, when I was excited. My Mom took me to the movies every night this was because my Dad owned the Washington Square Building, which housed the Kunsky movie theater and we could go to the movies free. I was so young and frightened that I'd grab my chin, and once I started this habit in my life, I couldn't stop myself.

I was desperate to overcome this bad habit. I often found myself in my usual prayer place at my Northwood home at the top of the stairs on the first landing with my head tucked into the first of the next steps going up. I was anxious to get rid of this habit and I knew only God could help me do it, so I ended my prayer to God with, "please give me something in place of it". He baptized me with His Holy Spirit. I was overwhelmed with the love of Jesus Christ. I did not know what I had, but I wanted to do cartwheels down the stairs and out the front door into the front yard. Instead I ran down the stairs and opened the front door and screen and did cartwheels into the yard and all around the front for hours. I did not know I could speak in tongues then, but I knew my life was changed.

Later on in my life I went forward for the baptism of the Holy Spirit as an adult, and I experienced the same overwhelming feeling of love of Jesus Christ again. I realized then what had happened to me so many years before.

I know I've had angels watching over me for many years, for I could have been killed so many times, but for His Divine helpers. I have often wondered what my purpose in life was. Perhaps it's just as the writer John Milton says, "They also serve who only stand and wait"; or it could be the writing of this book; or the painting I did of Father Coughlin. Only God knows, and that is sufficient for me.

One phenomenon that occurred in my life was the way I would hear a scripture aloud and then never forget it. I have always had a terrible time memorizing anything, but strangely the Scriptures stayed with me, though I did not realize then that they were from the Bible.

Later in life when I started to read the Bible I was shocked at all the Scriptures verses I knew. As a child, I also had a desire to go to church, so I would talk one of my girl friends usually Jeanne Johnson who wasn't Catholic into going to the Presbyterian Church with me. We would walk from our homes in the subdivision down to the Presbyterian Church south of 11mile road along Woodward Ave. My Dad was Presbyterian so it was only natural that I would go to his church. The people in the Church were so sweet to us.

We usually sat in the balcony area and would start to giggle, and invariably after the service, someone would tell us about the children's Sunday school class, which we were not at all interested in. I think this is where I learned most of the Scripture verses. I learned some from the movies that my Mom would take me to every night, like "Elmer Gantry" or "Sergeant York".

When I was no longer attending Shrine Grade School, during the summer, there was a time when Barbara Baldwin and I were walking along in front of my house on Northwood and we were pretending we were opera singers. We were singing our hearts out, in high falsetto voices. Across the street from the Shrine out from the rectory, Father Coughlin came running to catch up with us. He started to encourage us to join the choir and gave us the name of the person in charge of the choir and started to encourage us to join the choir. We were very flattered by his insistence, but we had no intention of going.

Chapter 3
Father Coughlin Liked FDR

When Franklin Delano Roosevelt was running for President in 1932, Father Coughlin was very popular on the air. My Dad was a strong Republican and favored Herbert Hoover, but the Great Depression was not improving. After the stock market crash in 1929 people were hurting everywhere in the country.

Building of the Charity of the Crucifixion Tower.

Father Coughlin had an extremely popular radio program. Radio was fairly new and there were no talk show hosts as there are today. His audience was in the millions, and even some of the Jewish people liked him. He was similar to our modern day Rush Limbaugh; he would explain the problems going on in Washington, DC. Many of his listeners were not Catholic, but he was a teacher and most Americans were Christians and at that time we called ourselves a Christian nation, which nobody doubted or questioned, (until the ACLU came into our country from Russia.) He would have little children answering questions he would ask them. Then he would say, "This little girl (or boy) knows the right solution. Why doesn't our Government"? I knew this because my sister was one of those children.

In those days we didn't have teachers telling us that George Washington was a Deist, or that we were not a Christian nation, or that Christians believed in three gods. That is what our public school system teaches now and what FDR brought into our country from Russia. However I am getting ahead of my story again. (I learned these statements from Social Study books when I was a substitute teacher in our Michigan Junior High school classes.)

When Hoover was running against FDR (Franklin Delano Roosevelt), Father Coughlin liked what Roosevelt had to say compared to the inaction of Hoover and he encouraged his listeners to vote for FDR. They became great buddies during that race, so much so that Father actually wrote FDR's Nomination Acceptance Speech. I know this because my friend Marian McCann's father waited the night of the nomination to hear which speech FDR would read, the speech writers or Father Coughlin's. Roosevelt's plane stopped in Detroit to pick up the one that Father had written. The answer came over the air waves that night, it was Father Coughlin's.

Charles J. Tull wrote in his book in 1965, "Father Coughlin and the New Deal," that Mrs. Eleanor Roosevelt said that Father Coughlin did not write Roosevelt's Inaugural Address, because, "He, (FDR), did not trust and disliked Coughlin from the beginning". He might not have liked Coughlin or trusted him, but he used Father Coughlin as much as he could. For Father had a tremendous gift of oratory and a wonderful voice and a naïve faith in his fellow man. Father was very trusting of FDR. He thought that this would be a "Change" that the country needed. Father could not endorse anyone, because of his faith, but he strongly disapproved of President Herbert Hoover actions. He talked admiringly of FDR.

The City of Royal Oak and the State of Michigan made Royal Oak one of their biggest branches of the Post Office because of the amount of mail arriving daily. Father had more than 500 workers just sorting out the mail at the Shrine and answering his mail. He put Royal Oak on the map. He felt so sorry for people who were down on their luck. He built the Shrine with the Scripture Jesus said, "If I be lifted up I will draw all men unto me".

The Shrine tower came into existence because the K.K.K. or the Black Legion or a similar group, burned a cross on the front lawn of the original little wooden church that had been there for some years. People from all over the United States would send nickels and dimes and quarters and pennies, to build a new church, during the hard depression years. Father had said that I will show "Christ to the World....not religion....but what we Catholics stand for, Jesus".

I truly believe that President Roosevelt would not have been elected if it had not been for Father Coughlin's encouragement to the American people that we needed a "new deal".

That was a term Father used a lot and it was picked up by the Roosevelt administration later on. I believe that Father changed the course of history with his vast audience. Just imagine someone like Rush Limbaugh or Sean Hannity pushing a candidate for this next election. They won't do it but if they were to be gung-ho for someone just think about what a difference the election would be! Father Coughlin was thrilled when FDR won the presidency but later he regretted it until his dying day.

Father felt so sorry for the hungry people that he opened up the fields next to the church and would feed all that he could. However, Royal Oak was quite a distance from Detroit so we did not see a huge crowd like the churches in Detroit saw. When Roosevelt had the farmers kill their pigs and cattle to keep the prices up Father was insensed. With all the starving people, how could Roosevelt do such a thing?

Years later I had the chance to talk with him in private about a few things that had stuck in my mind. He told me then, "During those years I felt that we could do no wrong. This is what God had called me to do to help the starving unhappy souls, to give them a chance in life, to help reform the government's thinking for the good of the people, not just the wealthy not just the poor, but for everyone. A new social order was needed, but the communists came in by way of "Franklin Double-crossing Roosevelt". I laughed when he said this because he was so quick and intense. "He really invited them into our State Department," he continued. "How could godless atheists possibly help us get out of a depression"? Instead they filled our public schools with socialistic and communistic philosophies. That's how they have taken over every country that they have been able to invade.

I wonder if it's realized that "the double-crosser" gave more than half the world away to the Soviets at the end of WWII (Yalta?). Did you notice that he gave the Catholic Christian nations away to the Russians who did little to win the war in the first place? We footed the Russians bill most of the way. We also had to watch our backs all through the war when they were around. At that time the Soviets wouldn't let people go freely out of their own countries and they were shot if they tried. That's what Roosevelt did for the world".

Believe it or not, the Soviets then continued to create problems for the free people of the world until President Reagan said "Mr. Gorbachev pull down this wall"! Oh how Father Coughlin would have loved President Reagan. Religion was once again flowing into the Christian nations and Pope John Paul II was head of the Roman Catholic Church. Even those people who were not Catholics loved this Pope. He looked upon the Jews as elder brothers in the Lord. They were all equal in Gods eyes. Pope John Paul II made everyone who saw him feel loved and accepted. I rather imagine that is how people felt about Jesus. That is the problem with religion. We start to put parameters around our beliefs and begin to exclude other people, and we lose our spontaneity and stifle the Holy Spirit.

There used to be a joke that went around about the Christian man who died and went to heaven. At the Pearly Gates St.Peter met him and started to show him around, when they came to a high stone wall the man said who is in there? "Shhh," said St. Peter, "Those are the Catholics," and they walked on further and there was another wall. Again St. Peter said, "Shhh, the Baptists". Soon they came to another wall and St. Peter said softly, "It's the Pentecostals... None of them think that anyone else is up here".

Chapter 4
Father Coughlin Disappointed in FDR

Most folks were elated when FDR made it into office, but soon after, Father Coughlin became disappointed when nothing seemed to be changing in Washington and FDR was utilizing all the programs Herbert Hoover had put into action and taking credit for them. Then the unthinkable happened that Father Coughlin could not get over. FDR invited Soviet intellectuals into our State Department to "help" out our depression problems.

Father would talk about it all the time, dwelling on the fact that President Roosevelt would do such a terrible thing as to invite those "Godless" communists into our country to contaminate our thinking. Just like Harry Reid would have loved to force Rush Limbaugh off the air, President Roosevelt wanted Father Coughlin off the air. However it was the Pope that forced Coughlin off the air with pressure from the Catholic friends of FDR. It was President Roosevelt's shenanigans again.

Archbishop Mooney was pressured by Catholic friends of President Roosevelt to threaten Father Coughlin that he had a choice to either get off the air waves or be defrocked. Archbishop Mooney was now his superior after Gallagher had died and being a good Catholic priest, Coughlin obeyed.

The communist propaganda in the USA called Father Coughlin a Jew hater. You must remember at that time in history, people in this country blamed the Jews for a lot of petty things. It was not only just in Germany but here in the States as well. I remember seeing signs at Walled Lake that said, "Gentiles Only". Deeds for houses said, "Not to be sold to any Jewish person", and country clubs like Red Run in Royal Oak had "no Jews are allowed to join," written in their rules. However, it wasn't Jews that Father Coughlin hated, it was the men like Lenin, and Marx, who created communism, and had denounced the God of Abraham, Isaac and Jacob to become atheistic communists.

He also disliked people like Stalin, who once believed in Christ but

116

later became an atheist and communist. I believe that Father Coughlin was a man ahead of his time. It took years for people to understand the horror of communism or socialism in our country. This seems to be trying to creep back into our government by way of our public school, brain-washed young people who want a "change".

Father Coughlin published a magazine called the Social Justice. My mother would never allow it into our house, because of her dislike for politics, so I really can't comment on the years leading to the war. I just know that he was a good priest.

He 'obeyed' those that had authority over him. He became silent after leaving the broadcasts and would only say things at Mass on Sundays. President Roosevelt was responsible for taking him off the air much to the sadness of the America people. Every Sunday at Mass in 1941, he would say something about his belief that we would be in war before the year was over. He was right. We were, as of December 7th 1941.

December 7th, 1941 was an infamous Sunday that I will never forget. Mother and I were on our way to guess what... the movies. We stopped off at the "Nelly Davis Drug Store". I turned on our car radio and they were announcing "Pearl Harbor," had just been attacked by Japanese bombers and that the President would be talking to us soon. President Roosevelt had been giving us a "Fireside Chat" once a week to keep us abreast as to what was going on about the Depression.

Now that Father Coughlin could no longer give his speech, President Roosevelt had the "air-ways" all to himself. No one else would go against the President and what he said. We had to stay united to show a strong front to Europe. No patriotic American would dare to criticize anything that President Roosevelt said all "patriotic citizens" must do.

The War was the only reason we got out of the Great Depression, not any of President Roosevelt's later plans. American factories came alive again but it took awhile because some of the businesses had closed down completely. Those people who could bring their business out of mothballs were able to make millions because of the War.

Everyone had a job and not enough were joining the army so conscription (some people called it the "draft") came into effect. All men eighteen-years old or older were getting letters from the government for them to report to the draft board and join the army that is if you weren't

4F, which was designated as physically unfit. The young men felt that it was a disgrace to be 4 F.

My cousin, Albert Pingree Herzog II, who had poor eyesight, would rather have died than to be classified 4 F, so he memorized the entire eye chart before he went for his physical and of course hid his glasses. He was accepted as 1A.

FDR put a clamp on everything. There would be absolutely no information given out except the propaganda that he felt was advantageous to the American people. We were constantly reminded that "a loose lip might sink a ship". We were told there were spy's all around us.

All the Japanese people were rounded up and put in "concentration camps", (we were told it was for their protection) and some of the Germans too. However, they didn't call them concentration camps, but some kind of "detention center". Minuro Yamosaki, the great architect, (the man who designed the World Trade Center that was destroyed on 9-11, 2001, in New York) and his family were placed in one during World War II.

There was only encouraging propaganda, only information that lifted up the spirits of the American people, even though we heard daily of thousands of our men dying in the fronts all over the world. We were still winning and were encouraged to help in any way we could, like saving bond drives and collecting used tires because someone might be able to use them. We surely couldn't buy any new ones, but they could retread the old ones. Gas and food ration books were distributed.

Instead of product advertisements on the bus walls we had war reminders like "A loose lip might sink a ship". Reminders were common like, "Beware of traitors. You may have spies all around you", or "Join the Navy, or "Become a Marine, Uncle Sam needs you". My family had a generous amount of French/German/Alsace-Lorraine, immigrants who spoke broken English and at times some of them were under scrutiny. My Dad had to intercede for them, because at that time he was a Commissioner of Royal Oak.

My Mom's family received many pleas from the Jewish organizations around the world because even though they considered themselves' Catholics they had a Jewish last name, Herzog. Since they were not Jewish they threw the letters away. They did not know how horrible the Jews were being treated.

Silver Jubilee June 29, 1941. Marian's the last girl
on the right in the white brimmed hat

We were young and eager to serve our country because we were a Christian nation and proud of it, and we needed to get out of the doldrums that the Depression had brought upon us. We knew we would "win the war to end all wars", for the "Old Country", where most of our ancestors had come from, because they needed our help. The "Great Depression" had molded us into God fearing people: No atheists were found in foxholes. We knew that life could change forever in an instant. Yes, God had shaped us to "trust in Him and not lean upon our own understanding, but in all our ways to acknowledge Him and He would direct our paths. (Proverbs 3:5, 6)

All of us had to sacrifice to help the war effort and most did so gladly. That meant that we had to have "Ration Cards," for everything we bought like: sugar, flour, eggs, meat and gasoline. You could not buy any more than your coupons allowed, but you could borrow from your family or friends...so "black market" came into the American market place. Naturally everyone closely guarded their stamps.

Gas rationing was on an A, B or C stamp basis. "A" gave you a little gas, "B" gave you a little more and "C" gave you the most gas you could get. You could not get any extra unless you were an air raid warden, or someone in another vital position.

You could not get anything extra, because everything went into the war effort. No tennis balls, no golf balls, or tees were available. Television was unheard of until after the war, but we did listen to our radio as much as possible.

A lot of the women got jobs to relieve the men for service. "Rosie the Riveter" came into songs and our lives. Women seldom got jobs, before the war especially assembly line jobs. Only office jobs were available to them, unless your family owned a small factory, and they would bring parts home to assemble on the kitchen table. (My friend Rosemary DeWolf's family used to do this.)

My Aunt Lula went over to Canada and would smuggle all the meat she wanted. The Canadians had no rationing like we did, but you couldn't buy any of the rationed items there and bring them back into the States. Nobody stopped my Aunt Lula. When she had "a bee in her bonnet" there was no stopping her. It was easy to go to Canada from Detroit. We did it all the time. It was easier than going to Ohio, because it was closer.

Chapter 5
Tragedy in Our Lives

Then the tragedy in our lives came on February 8th, 1944. We received a telegram from the War Department that my brother, Lt. Lloyd Firman Clawson was killed in a training demonstration in England with Eisenhower, Churchill, and all the allied leaders who were preparing for D-Day. They had introduced a basket to be dropped out of the plane before the paratroopers, and in Buddy's case it hit the stabilizer and the plane couldn't go up or down and crashed. They never used that basket again according to one of the pilots.

Father came over to our house along with half of our Royal Oak neighbors. He made the mistake of telling a lady in his church who I called the "Town Crier" that "now Val (my Mom) will come back to the church". When my Mom heard that she said, "Never".

As a family we went through the rest of the war torn apart. My sister had a "breakdown" and in someway felt responsible for her brother's death. You have to remember, in those days no one knew very much about mental stress or mental illness.

The closest things the doctors could tell us had to do with the men from World War I and "Shell Shock". We knew nothing about "brain washing" at that time. Freud was someone people didn't understand. He was hung up on sex, and our psychologists on shock treatments. While we were searching into Freudian concepts the communists were into Pavlov and his conditioning theories. Thus we couldn't understand why our boys in "The Korean War" were chanting and reciting communist propaganda when they were captured. Our psychologists had so much to learn, because they were so focused on Freudian concepts and shock treatments, but were not considering conditioning theories.

Our boys were such good kids that many believed the propaganda they were told. The communists spoke to them as if they were their friends and would say things like, "We don't have much food but we will share all we have with you". Then they would begin to pit one soldier against another and cause discord. They would start playing recordings to them that were filled with propaganda about how horrible America was. The fellows who believed them would be given more food and the ones who argued that America was good would get very little or no food. This would start a fight between the GI prisoners and would cause great confusion among the men so that some of them just went to bed and pulled the covers over their heads and died for no known physical reason.

Our doctors were shocked to hear of this. They had a lot to learn. The Army began to teach our soldiers how to resist the enemy properly no matter how nice the enemy was to them. They were still the enemy.

After World War II we learned about all the horrors of the Nazi extermination camps and the treatment of the Jewish people. The news that we received was always about our armed forces and how many thousands of young men we had lost that day in battle. Then after the war we began to see the newsreels about the death camps in the European countries that the Germans captured.

Hearing things like "lamp shades" made from the skin, bones and teeth of those poor Jewish people was a terrible shock to us and this only came to us after the war was over. How one nation that was supposedly so educated could have become so Barbaric was beyond our comprehension.

It was so horrendous we knew it was not propaganda. The people of the world felt so guilty because they could remember all the jokes and maligning they had done before the Holocaust.

Before the war, the Jewish people were often treated like "scape goats" for other people's emotions, and problems. It was irrational thinking, but less painful to blame problems on others then to look for the cause within themselves; instead of blaming them on yourself. Even if they didn't know any Jewish people, it was all right to blame them. This thinking had to go. Jealousy may have played a big part in this attitude.

Some were smarter, and had more money, and they were "God's Chosen People". Deuteronomy 7: 6-8 "For thou art an holy people unto the Lord thy God; the Lord thy God hath chosen thee to be a special people unto himself, above all people that are upon the face of the earth. The Lord did not set his love upon you, nor chose you, because you were more in number than any people; for you were the fewest of all people:

But because the Lord loved you; and because he would keep the oath which he had sworn unto your fathers......"

In 1948 Israel became a nation again just as God had told the prophets of old, so the Bible again foretold the world's future. (Acts1:7) In 1948, God also gave the Jewish people, Jerusalem, as evidenced by the "Six Day War" and then God rested on the SEVENTH day. (Gen.2:2) For about two thousand years the Jewish people would always say after their Passover meal, "Next year Jerusalem"!

After WWII Americas laws and attitudes toward any underdog began to change for the better. Polish people weren't called "Polock's", or Jews "Hymies," or Italians "Whops" or Irish "Shanty Irish" or Black Americans "Niggers" or Chinese "Chinks" any more. Now the only name calling was against the original founding fathers. They were called WASP's (White Anglo-Saxon Protestants.) Hay....I'm a WASP and I don't blame others for my defaults or faults.....I did them all by myself. Jesus forgives me and that's what really counts.

Chapter 6
Peace Came into Our Lives

After the Korean War we had peace for a little while. My friends and I were now getting married and starting out on new adventures of our own. On July 9th 1953, my friend Marian McCann was married to her long time boy friend, Johnny Rometty. He adored her and they had six wonderful children.

When she and Johnny were married I had a chance to meet Father Coughlin again, because he officiated at her wedding.

Things sometimes go wrong at weddings but nothing like it did at Marian's. We were all sitting for what seemed like hours. Father had been fiddling around with the little things on the altar and looking busy. The organist was playing music, and ad-libbing over and over. We were all glancing around for the bride or her father, but there was no sign of them. Then the organist started the wedding march and Marian's bridesmaids started coming down the aisle, and we all stood up. Johnny looked relieved and the bride had forgotten to pull her veil over her head and was rushing down the aisle with her dad.

Father Coughlin had been waiting up at the altar for at least an hour and he had known Marian and her Irish family since he first became the priest at the Shrine of the Little Flower. When Father started to talk he could really talk about anything and everything, and no one was dismissed to sit down. In the middle of the service, I remember him talking about the Cuneiform Clay Tablets found in the sand in Egypt. I don't know what this had to do with their marriage. But he was going to make them wait as he had waited. For at least another forty-five minutes he talked and Marian's bridesmaids were swaying like palm trees in a wind storm. They looked like they were going to faint. Finally he finished the service.

After it was all over, all of us had a good laugh because everyone in the bride's family was at the church, but no one remembered to pick up the bride and her father. Each one thought the other had brought them.

In 1964, I had painted a picture of my Dad, H. Lloyd Clawson and my baby daughter Annette. She would come home from Roeper Pre-school and crawl up in his lap and fall asleep (During that time we saw the death of JFK and Lee Harvey Oswald on television) I did another painting of Annette with her cat. She loved to dress this cat up. She named her cat after a counselor she loved at Roepers School named Lois Berman…so I called the painting "Annette and Lois Berman". I also painted a passionate picture of Jackie Kennedy with her husband JFK in her lap. When I was finished I was surprised to see what looked like a red devil was in it, which I had never intended to put in.

Grandpa Lloyd Clawson with his Granddaughter Annette circa 1964.

I was doing a lot of painting at that time and I wanted to paint Father Coughlin so I called and went over to see him. He said he would love to have me paint his portrait. So we made arrangements for me to come back another day and do some sketches. During those times I was able to ask questions about religion, faith and all kinds of things

I had always wanted to know. The sketches were done as he read his newspaper.

He later sent me a Photograph of himself with a short haircut and asked me to eventually return it to him. I did not like his looks with short hair, but I said nothing, but, "Thanks".

Chapter 7
One of the Finest Priests Who Ever Lived

I wish to express very carefully to you my reader that I consider Father Coughlin the Royal Oak priest, to be one of the finest men that ever lived. You may respond by saying that he was an anti-Semite and hated the Jews. No....No... He hated the communists and the fascists, and he felt that the communists were the worst. Remember that Socialism is the same as Communism, however, Socialism achieves its goals in a slower fashion, but the same goals and results.

He said that communism was started by Jews, such as, Lenin, Marx, etc. and that he couldn't understand how they would give up the God of Abraham, Isaac, and Jacob, to be atheists. He never wanted to get into politics, but was drawn into it by circumstances. He thought that President Roosevelt was an answer to prayer for the hurting people until FDR, invited the communists into our State Department to "help" us get out of the Great Depression.

He talked about how wrong it was for godless men to give us the answers, to our problems. He regretted some of the terrible things that he had said in the heat of a teaching about communism and his Jewish remarks and his influence in electing President Roosevelt. He felt that if he had stayed out of politics, President Hoover would have been elected again.

I told him that I believed he helped change history. I believe the Lord directed his statements. We would have turned very communistic if he had not warned the American people about the communist agenda and the fact that they were in Mexico persecuting the priests and nuns and the Catholic Church forcing them to marry or be killed as was his friend, Father Pro, the Jesuit martyr , and the churches turned into museums owned by the government. The Scripture tells us that, "The steps of a righteous man are ordered by the Lord". (Proverbs 16) even if we don't like the results.

The communists in this country have vilified Father Coughlin's name so much that people, particularly Jewish people, think that he was an anti-Semite, and a Jew hater. To my dear Jewish friends and relatives I emphatically want you to know that was not true. At that time in history every one was against someone and the Jews became the scapegoat, particularly with some of them starting communism. Father Coughlin was against some of the things the Jewish bankers and communist were doing, but not against the Jewish people.

If circumstances had been different and he had been from Poland, he might have died in the gas chambers too because he was so much against mistreatment of his fellow man. He never could have been silent under those conditions. He was a hot headed young Irishman, who mellowed some with age. He was an isolationist, and wanted America to stay out of the war. We had many isolationists in our country at that time.

Years later Father and I discussed this briefly and tears came into his eyes and he said it was hard to believe that human beings could be so cruel to one another. I countered by using the Scripture from St John (John 10:10). There is still a devil, who "is out to kill, steal and to destroy". He hates all of us because God came to give us Life. People that don't know God don't know what we are talking about. Jesus said, "I HAVE COME TO GIVE YOU LIFE AND LIFE MORE ABUNDANTLY".

I've met ministers in the Protestant churches who became pastors of their denomination because they liked doing nice things for people, but they don't know Jesus personally. They know about Him but they don't know Him personally. You know when you have a personal relationship with Him. Each of us has a different testimony to tell of when we met Him personally and when we were called to do His work. "Yes," Father said to me, "That happened to me as a boy and I can tell you when it happened to me and where I was. That is really a strange remembrance. I hadn't thought of that in years". (I wish I had asked him to tell me more about it at that time).

At that point I told him how I met the Lord. I also told him about the class where we heard the story about a little girl who was used by God. Sister asked us to put our heads down and to think about whether we wanted God to use us as a child or as an adult. I said to the Lord, "Use me when I am older Lord, but I don't want to be a nun".

I loved my nuns but I didn't want to be one. He and I laughed at my childishness. You don't tell God what you don't want to be. Years later I said to myself I don't want to be a hair designer or take care of old folks, and wouldn't you know it those are the two businesses God put me in, and I loved them both.

Father told me the Lord chose him to come to Royal Oak. He said he really trembled when he was told because he did not want to take the vows of poverty or go to a primitive nation, but he would go if the Lord wanted that. He was not a maverick, but an obedient priest all his life.

He believed strongly in obedience to those who had charge over him. Bishop Gallagher, his superior, was proud of him and encouraged him to say the things that he said about changing the government's way of helping the American people. Father Coughlin wrote scathing remarks about dissident priests and bishops in his later year, citing how the priests of the 1960's were wrong in their attitudes against the Pope. He castigated the errant bishops for not controlling their rebellious priests who speak out against the Holy See. His strong feelings of injustice came out in his book, "The Bishops Versus the Pope". He was a man of strong convictions of right and wrong and vociferously spoke out against what he deemed to be wrong.

We discussed the gift of oratory that God had given him. I said that he had used it well. He said that he was always remorseful for helping President Roosevelt get elected instead of President Hoover, because he now thought President Hoover was a good man. And I told him about the class I took at Oakland University in which my professor said that Hoover lived long enough to have been exonerated from any wrong doing as President. He said that he had a chance to meet with President Hoover years later and that he apologized to him.

I said that I have learned that trials, tribulations, and errors are a part of our life and we "should not lean upon our own understanding but in all our ways acknowledge God and He will direct our paths". That's a favorite scripture of mine. We don't have any way of knowing that the way we take or took was not directed of the Lord. Only God knows. All we know is that it didn't break his commandments and was never done to hurt but to help. (Proverbs 3)

I have attempted to set the record straight, so that people will stop vilifying Father Coughlin and pray that his message of staying away from communism takes hold in our country again. All we have to do is to look at Russia today and see what communism can do to a country. He was a teacher and he taught the American people from the radio much the same as Rush Limbaugh, Sean Hannity, Michael Reagan, and Glenn Beck are doing today. Radio was a powerful new commodity in those days and Father Coughlin was the only "Talk Show Host" we had at that time, even though "he was on loan from God", he was a human being who made mistakes.

We had a war in which the American men fought with moral convictions, because of the teachings of Father Coughlin. He taught them morals with common sense answers.

In 1964 Father Coughlin allowed Bernard Eismann of CBS News to interview him. Father Coughlin said, "Well I suppose I committed an egregious error which I am the first to admit when I permitted myself to attack persons. I could never bring myself to philosophize the morality of that now. It was a young man's mistake".

He also saw President Roosevelt as a change from that of Hoover's presidency and had faith that President Roosevelt would come up with a "new deal" for the American People. President Roosevelt took advantage of the priest's ability to get the Catholic vote and rode it to the hilt. Father Coughlin was naïve and thrilled with President Roosevelt's interest in him and misunderstood politics for a spirit of fellowship and camaraderie.

Father Coughlin was proud of knowing the President, and being used to write speeches for him, and thought that FDR saw things as he did for the good of the people. It was just politics for FDR. Father Coughlin was proud of being close to the President of the United States, and for a long time he defended him, but in 1935, when he saw that FDR was bringing "godless" atheists into our State Department he no longer could support him. He didn't want our government contaminated by the ideology of godless men. This is one of the biggest problems we have today in the twenty-first century.

Atheists and other politicians have to keep prayers out of our schools. The Democrats and some Republican used to be God fearing Americans but allowed prayers to be taken out of our schools when we were not looking. They now want to take "In God We Trust" off of our money. Unbelievably, they have tried to take God out of our United States Pledges of Allegiance. We the people, God fearing Democrats and Republicans, have to take charge over our State Department (government) to make sure they don't succeed.

In 1937 his beloved friend and mentor Bishop Gallagher died, and his successor Cardinal Mooney did not agree with Father Coughlin and wanted to put a lid on Father Coughlin and his remarks, because President Roosevelt's Catholic friends were pressing him to stop Father from speaking out. Cardinal Mooney threatened Father Coughlin that he would be defrocked if he did not give up his radio program. Father chose to follow his faith and be an obedient priest, but he still spoke his mind from the Altar.

The main reason Roosevelt won a third term was because nobody wanted to "change horses in mid stream". We were in a war and no one wanted to try someone new until the war was over. Later in life, Father Coughlin said that he thought that U.S. Presidents should not be criticized.

Chapter 8
Father Gave the Eulogy

In 1971, on July 16th my Dad H. Lloyd Clawson died at his beloved Beaumont Hospital in Royal Oak, Michigan. He had been a great man in Royal Oak politics for many years. He had a wonderful sense of humor and was loved by all who knew him.

We wondered who we would get to give his eulogy at Sullivan and Sons funeral home in Royal Oak. Dad had not attended any church since I had married and moved away. My Dad had been totally blind for several years and none of the pastors in Royal Oak knew him well enough to say a few words over his coffin, I suggested that Father Coughlin might be willing to speak because by then I had renewed my friendship with him.

I had gone to see Father at his home in Birmingham for I had wanted to do an oil painting of him. I also wanted to share with him the fact that I was "born again" as Jesus said that we must be to SEE the Kingdom of God, St John 3: 3. He was so happy for me. He made no attempt to get me back into the Catholic Church, and we discussed Scripture every time we got together. In the mean time I was doing some sketches, but I spent more time discussing the Bible and talking than sketching. The sketches were for a future oil painting I would do of him. He saw my work and liked them.

He told me that he had chosen himself a new lawyer, "Police Chief Hayward's son". I told him that Jack was our class president at Royal Oak High in 1945 and that he was smart and a nice honest man.

My Dad's death was very painful for all of us. My son William had the opportunity to pray with Dad on his deathbed. I mentioned to my Mom that Father Coughlin might be willing to say the eulogy. My Mom had been so provoked over his involvement in politics that I was not at all sure whether she would accept this suggestion, but she heartily agreed to have him.

Father came to the funeral parlor and I was going to tape the whole message and I put the recorder in my purse and nothing was taped. I had hoped that someone else had recorded it, but I have never found anyone so I have to rely on my memory.

I felt as if he was talking to me about some of the things we had talked about, because I had discovered Jesus outside of the Catholic Church. I had told him that I had known about Jesus in the heavens or outside of me, but did not know that God wanted me to invite Him to come into my body, until I read Revelation 3: 20. "Behold I stand at the door and knock: if any man hears my voice, and opens the door, I will come into him, and will sup with him and he with me".

Then I read in Colossians1:26 & 27, "The mystery that has been hid from ages and generations, is now made manifest to his saints; To whom God would make known what is the riches of the glory of this mystery among the Gentiles; which is Christ IN you, the hope of Glory".

I told Father I would always consider myself a Catholic, but that the church probably would not. I didn't care because Jesus loved me even if the Church didn't. I not only considered myself a Catholic, but a Presbyterian, a Lutheran, a Congregationalist or any of the other churches that believed in the Nicene Creed and the Apostles Creed.

At the funeral home Father began to talk about the Council of Nicaea in 325 A.D. which Constantine had brought together after becoming a "believer" in Jesus Christ, because at that time there were so many factions, and Constantine insisted on one creed for Christianity. The leaders of the day were having a hard time coming up with a creed that all who were true believers could accept. Then finally a young lad came forth and put it all into words that the council could accept. Thus the Nicene Creed came into existence.

I felt Father Coughlin was giving me a teaching about early Christianity, because there were a lot of different beliefs at that time, as there is now and it was a tremendous decision to formulate a definite creed that all could believe. This separated the Gnostics and other sects who claimed to be Christians, but were in error, from those who believed the truth.

As we know today, there are different factions or groups which call themselves Christian but they are not. The Muslims claim that Allah is God, but to Christians and Jews he is not. For Christians and Jews believe in the God of Abraham, Isaac, and Jacob, but the Muslims believe in the god of Abraham, Ishmael, and Nebajoth. There are other religions that believe in their gods, which is their choice, but they are not the Christian God or the Jewish God.

Christians must believe that Jesus Christ was and is the Living Son of God. Jesus Himself told His disciples when they came to Him and said, "Master we saw one casting out devils in your name, and he follows not us, and we forbade him". And Jesus said, "Forbid him not; for there is no man who shall do a miracle in my name, that can lightly speak evil of me. For he that is not against us is on our side".(Mark 9: 38-40 King James)

Father talked about the contributions my Dad had given to so many people and to Royal Oak and the church also how much he was loved and would be missed, saying, "There is neither male or female, Greek or Jew but that we are all one in Christ Jesus". This I recognized as Scripture, and I thought that he said this because my father was not a Catholic.

My son William gave the prayer at the gravesite because Father could not go there. He talked about his grandpa and when he had prayed with him in the hospital as he was dying. He said that tears came into his eyes and he knew that Dad had heard. His grandson went on to become a minister.

Shortly after the funeral I went to see Father again at his house in Birmingham. As I was sketching I started talking to Father about the Charismatic renewal that was going on at the Shrine on Tuesday nights and how much I enjoyed taking people there. I also told him about the Holy Spirit meetings at St. Sylvester's Catholic Church in Warren, led by Frank Majewski. We talked for a while about the Charismatic renewal that was sweeping the Catholic, Methodist, Episcopalian, and Lutheran churches in the late 1960 an early 1970's.

I told him about the time I took our youth pastor's wife from the first Presbyterian Church in Birmingham and her sister, who was a Wycliff Bible translator just back from South America to the Charismatic renewal meeting at the Shrine Church Tower. As we began to sing I started to sing in glossolalia or tongues as the Bible calls it. Both of my visitors stopped singing in English and when we went to sit down they asked me if I spoke Spanish and I said, "Very little". They said, "We didn't think you did, but you were singing praises to God in the most intricate forms of Spanish". This was a miracle that happened right there at the St. Therese' Tower, and I didn't know it was any different than any other time I sang to God in tongues.

I also mentioned how one time I was praying with a young man after Frank Majewski had an "altar call" and found out later that he was from the Shrine. I had the opportunity to pray with his father too. His father shared with me that his son had been addicted to heroin and The Lord had set him free from the addiction with no side effects. I was so surprised to hear of this, but the Lord wanted to bless me with this information.

I told him of the testimony of an ex-Hells Angel or biker that had a prayer meeting in Warren. His name was Frank Majewski, who was an orphan raised in a Catholic orphanage. He and his brother were later adopted by a lovely family, but his life was scarred. He would tell everyone how he met Jesus personally and how his life had changed at the ripe old age of 20 years old after he had been shot in the face.

The priest that he had known as a boy had given him permission to use the Social hall to tell what had happened to him. Hundreds of people were flocking to his meetings every Friday night. Doctors, lawyers, and young people from off the street, all were being born again by the power of his testimony. I was thrilled with it and wanted to take Father over to hear him. However, regretfully, I never had the opportunity.

I mentioned to Father that I was concerned that my Mom did not know Jesus. I told him that she was not a believer, that she did not know Jesus as God and Lord. He said to me, "You bring her over here. I would love to see her again, and I will show you she is a good Catholic". I told my mom and she set a date for us to go and see him.

We arrived at his front door and he answered the doorbell. He said, "Hello Val, how are you? And Therese, how are you"? I nodded and Mom said, "I'm fine, and how are you Charley"? He told us to come in and sit down. They chatted a bit about past friends and happenings and I decided to get to the point. I said, "Father, my Mom does not believe in Jesus Christ as God". He said, "Sure you do. Don't you Val? You're a good Catholic". Her reply almost knocked him off his chair. She said, "Now Charley, you know that he was just a smart Jew"! He said in a moaning way, "VAL" He tried to say more but backed off and said to me, "I'm going to say a Mass every Sunday for her and you keep praying too". I said, "Thank you, I know prayer works". All of my life I had always heard her say that same statement. That ended our visit.

In 1978, I went through a divorce and I never saw Father Coughlin again for he went to be with the Lord in 1979. I put his portrait on hold until 2008 when I finally finished it.

When Father passed away, my Mom had not yet met Jesus and I was never able to tell him or see him again. Mom finally "saw the "Light" so to speak, and asked Jesus into her life before she passed away six years later. She finally knew He was much more than a 'smart' Jew, He was the Word of God made flesh and dwelt among us, as St. John said in the first chapter of his Gospel. I had pointed out to her that He, Jesus, was a good man and not a liar. At last she did understand this.

Jesus had been sent by God to break the power that the devil had over mankind. The devil knew that God was planning something, but he didn't know what it was. The evil one also knew that he could not touch Jesus, because God had given His angels charge over Him to keep Him in all His ways (Luke 4:10), until Jesus' time on earth had come to an end. The devil thought he had won against God when he had crucified Jesus. Then he realized he had killed the Lord of Glory and to all who believed in Him He gave them eternal Life; to be in Heaven with Him, Jesus, the Word of God (1Cor. 2:8).

I told Mom about the revelation the Lord had given me when I asked Him in prayer to reveal the Trinity in the Old Testament, because the New Testament is supposed to be the same as the Old Testament only revealed. People say that Christians worship three gods. That is wrong! We worship one God. "Hear this O Israel, the Lord our God is one". I knew of examples like Joseph or David, who were types of the Messiah (Christ is the Greek word for Messiah) but I had never heard what God taught me that day. People would try and explain the Trinity like an egg with the yoke, albumin, and shell.

When, God opened up the eyes of my understanding He said to me, "Turn to Genesis, chapter one, verse one, and read it to me", so I immediately turned and read, "In the beginning God..." He said, "Stop, what does verse two say"? I read, "And the earth was without form and void and darkness was upon the face of the deep. And the Spirit of God... "Stop", He said. "So now you have God in the first verse and His Spirit in the second verse. Now read verse three "And God said... "Stop, do you understand? You have a spirit and you speak your words. I have a Spirit and I Speak My Words. You cannot separate Me from My Word, My Word and I Am One".

"St John saw this when he wrote the first verse of his Gospel. 'In the beginning was the Word and the Word was with God and the Word was God.' My spoken Word came and dwelt among you. My Son was manifested to destroy the works of the devil. He came to set you free by His obedience to My spoken Word. He did not lie. He is the Truth. He said to the woman at Jacob's well, 'I am the Messiah, called Christ'. (John 4:25, 26)"

I told all of this to my Mom and I said, "We are made after God's likeness (Genesis 1:26). Mom we have a body, soul (which includes your mind will and emotions) and a spirit. How we use our mind, will, and emotions, is by speaking our words. That is precisely what God has done by giving us the Bible. Jesus has revealed His Soul for us, to try and be more like Him. He has given us his Word. His living Word is alive today.

The Apostles wanted to know when Israel would be a Kingdom again (Acts 1:6), and Jesus told them it was not for Him to say, because only the Father knew that. Yet in our lifetime we saw this miracle take place, 1948. That is why I can say I believe the Bible to be the LIVING word of God. The Jews for hundreds of years had been saying at their Passover meal, "Next year Jerusalem". That miracle happened when they won possession of Jerusalem in the "Six Day War".

The reason the devil hates the Jews and Christians is because God loves them so much. Anyone who hates the people of God is being used by the devil to sow discord, and God hates anyone who sows discord in His Church. God calls them an abomination

(Proverbs 6: 19).

"Always, search your heart Mom, and be honest with yourself. If there is anything you find in your life that you don't like, ask Jesus to take it away. It won't be painful when He does. Just ask Him".

The Scripture says, "You don't receive because you do not ask and when you do ask, you ask amiss". She nodded her head in agreement and said the "sinners prayer" with me for the second time, (The first time she was angry with me for nagging her and said it to dismiss me.) This time she did it meaningfully. "Jesus," she said, "Come into my life and be my Lord and forgive all my sins". From then on she would ask me to pray for her every time I went to see her. She passed away in Beaumont Hospital. She was 95 years old.

The Shrine of the Little Flower is not an edifice to St Therese. It is an edifice in honor of Jesus Christ whom she loved. Throughout the entire building you will find that all of the words are there to glorify Jesus Christ. I truly enjoyed my trip through the church that Father Coughlin built during the Great Depression years. The beautiful Art Deco that was delicately captured throughout the structure is breath taking. I must acknowledge the tour when Linda Penney took me through, with the help of the Church's guide, Karen Neilson. They shared many important pieces of data, and I thank them from the bottom of my heart.

If only all Christian Americans would emphasize to people that we do not worship our churches, but we worship Him, Jesus the Son of God, the Word made Flesh that dwelt among us (St. John I: 14). That is why we are called Christians because we worship Him. We must get back to the basics of our Bible. It is the PEOPLE that make up the Church of Jesus Christ and not the buildings.

Some church groups are the eyes of Jesus, some are the ears, some are the arms, some are the hands, some are the feet but all together they make up the body and Church of our Lord.

That is why when any Christian group is attacked by any hostile force we should all loudly disapprove the action and continue noisily rebuking the incident until it is resolved to our liking. The Bible says that the meek or humble will inherit the earth (Ps37:11), not the WHIMPS.

Remember that God said, "Moses was very meek, above all men upon the face of the earth" (Num.12: 3). I have discovered in talking to various people that the people who get the angriest at the Catholic Church are ex Catholics. It is not the Churches fault that you did not meet Jesus while you were there. It might have been a designed plan of God. I know it was not the Churches fault, but yours. Jesus said, "Seek and you will find"(Matt 7:7). He doesn't lie!

As united Christians, we should speak out loudly to the World even if those who are being persecuted are not from our particular denomination. They are part of His Body and we should stand up and be counted. "God does not give the spirit of fear but of power love and a sound mind".(2nd Tim 1: 7) Our only fear should be in disobeying

God. Not whether the world hates us ...so what else is new? We are in the world not of the world. (1 John 2:15-17) We are Christians, Gods peculiar people (1 Pet 2:9). Just as the Jews are God's peculiar people (De 26:18). Don't shoot me down for what I say, but let it ride for we all believe in the same God, the God of Abraham, Isaac and Jacob. He founded the Church.

We are not God and we have to believe His Word and stop playing God. We are to love Him with all our heart, soul, mind and strength (Matt 22:37).

Christians have to stop being afraid, but stand up and be counted. We are in a battle and too many are afraid to be "politically incorrect", when we allow Hollywood to depict Christians, monks, priests and ministers as evil. We must fight back. I do not like the Hollywood movies that use the name of Jesus Christ as a swear word, because it is offensive to Christians.

The wonderful nature of the Jewish people is that they defend other Jews even if they do not agree with them, because they are Jewish. Why aren't Christians more like that, defending other Christians? Jesus admonished us saying "Love one another as I have loved you, (John 13: 34, 35) by this shall all men know that you are my disciples, if you have love one to another".

The Catholic and other Christian denominations can no longer be "politically correct" and back away from communism and the enemies of our day. They must face and fight them as Father Charles E. Coughlin did communism. There is only one God. He is the God of Abraham, Isaac and Jacob and His Words name is Jesus Christ whether you like it or not. There is no in between, if you know Him you know that I am right but if you don't know Him you will try and look for another way.

Christians have to stop fighting among themselves. I see this happening more and more with the Christians trying to solve the world's problems by entering into them.

I believe that God has a different plan for the Jewish unbelievers, who will someday as it says in Zechariah 12: 8-10, "In that day shall the Lord defend the inhabitants of Jerusalem; and he that is "feeble" among them at that day shall be as David; and the house of David shall be as God, as the Angel of the Lord before them. (Vs 9) And it shall come to pass in that day, that I will seek to destroy all the nations that come against Jerusalem. (Vs 10) And I will pour upon the house of David, and upon the inhabitants of Jerusalem, the spirit of grace and of supplications: and they shall look upon me whom they have pierced, and they shall mourn for him, as one mourns for his only son, and shall be in bitterness for him, as one that is in bitterness for his only son". And that will be done in Gods time.

Father Charles E. Coughlin was a man ahead of his times, but he is relevant even now in the twenty first century. I love the State of Michigan and I see God's winter hand on Michigan. As the nun said to me as a child, "Don't let the devil steal God from you". I say this to Michiganders and the Bible says to us His people, "Look up your redemption is drawing nigh"
(Luke 21: 28).

THE END OF AN ERA?

About the Author

Therese M. Christman "is amazing" say, the people that know her. She personifies the hope and quest of the American dream. Her life accomplishments excel from the ultra practical to the unbelievable. You might see her on a rooftop constructing along with her husband. Maybe you will listen to her in the lecture hall expounding biblical principles. You may encounter her at a political event where she passionately fights for the convergence of conservative values in America's social structure. This is just a small sampling of her profile that shapes the wonder of this amazing woman.

Therese Christman is well educated with studies at the University of Michigan and Oakland University. She earned her degree with majors in history, psychology and social studies. She translated her educational achievements into becoming a very successful business owner. Along with her talented husband she became co-founder and director of the Christman Assisted Living Facility in Royal Oak, Michigan.

When people engage her on a social level, they are greeted with a smile and a charisma that touches those vital areas of one's heart. Therese Christman permeates energy that transcends leaving you renewed and blessed in that moment of sharing with her.

Her love for a city and a father who played a major role in shaping its foundations, coupled with having a famous priest as a close friend, explains why this book, "The Mayor's Daughter", defined as a trilogy of the 20th century, was a passionate calling for her to author. This is a compelling true story of her memories, of an internationally renowned Catholic priest and her father, an icon of business and civic affairs in Royal Oak, Michigan. This book is a must read!